# THE Daredevil BOOK FOR Golfers

# THE Daredevil BOOK FOR Golfers

## Cunning Strategies To Tee Up Your Game

TIM GLYNNE-JONES

ILLUSTRATED BY DAVID MOSTYN

ARCTURUS

**Tim Glynne-Jones** is a journalist and sporadic golfer living and shanking in the UK. His writing career has covered a range of subjects, including music, motoring, sport and food, and in the last couple of years he has written *The Book of Numbers* and *The Book of Words*, both for Arcturus. If he could improve one thing about his golf, it would be his score at the end of each round.

Illustrator **David Mostyn** began his career as a commercial artist in advertising, then moved into publishing and set up his own company Mostyn Partners in 1977. David has worked for 30 years in comic strips, producing drawings for DC Thomson, Marvel Comics and DC Comics, among others. He is married with two children and a cat, and lives in Oxford. This is his third Daredevil book.

ARCTURUS

This edition published in 2010
by Arcturus Publishing Limited
26/27 Bickels Yard,
151–153 Bermondsey Street,
London SE1 3HA

ISBN: 978-1-84837-545-1
AD001473EN

Printed in China

# CONTENTS

# INTRODUCTION

Forget all the other golf books you've read, this is the only one you will ever need. Most golf books focus on one aspect of the game, as if getting one thing right will make all the other bits fall into place. Of course, golf doesn't work like that, as I know only too well. This book tackles every single aspect of golf, from the pattern on your trousers to the way you should grip your club when throwing it. And because I've experienced all the lows golf has to offer, and lived to tell the tale, you know that the advice I give comes from hard-earned experience, not some theory concocted with your publisher while polishing your claret jug between tournaments. As a wise man once said, 'Those who can can't teach', or something like that.

Hi. My name's Barty Thickett and I'm a compulsive golfer. There, that's got that off my chest. If you'd like to make the same confession, you've come to the right place. What do I have in common with Tiger Woods? Not a lot, except we both have surnames that mean 'a collection of trees' (actually it's pronounced thi-kett). I have never won the Masters, although I dream about it sometimes, as you'll find out later. (In fact, I've never won any of the majors – the Masters just happened to be the first one I thought of.)

But, like Tiger, I spend a lot of time pondering golf. In fact, I think about little else. When you travel the world's golf courses by yourself, with just a set of clubs, an outrageous wardrobe and a collection of elaborate gadgets for company, there's not much to occupy your mind. The upshot is that I have developed my own bulletproof philosophy.

***Barty Thickett's Golfing Philosophy...***

IF YOU WANT TO WIN AT GOLF, FIRST YOU MUST WIN IN YOUR OPPONENT'S MIND

I've read other golfing philosophies, all of which seem a bit odd. Take these two, for instance:

GOLF IS A GAME PLAYED AGAINST YOURSELF

Correct me if I'm wrong, but I don't believe a major has ever been contested between just one player and his alter ego. Maybe I missed it. Maybe there was an occasion when The Open went to a play-off between Dr Jekyll and Mr Hyde. But I'm sure such instances are rare.

## YOU DON'T PLAY YOUR OPPONENT, YOU PLAY THE COURSE

OK, so you play the course and you beat it, but if everyone else does the same, where does that leave you? Back where you started.

No, I've studied the records and I can safely say that in order to win at golf you have to beat other people. There are two ways to do this:

1. BE A BETTER GOLFER THAN THEY ARE

2. PUT THEM RIGHT OFF THEIR GAME

Given the unpredictable nature of golf, and the conditions in which it's played, it seems obvious that the latter is the more sensible course to follow.

I have dedicated my life to mastering the psychological side of the game, working out ways to get inside my opponent's head and unhinge him. It doesn't take much, as you'll learn when you read through this book.

To get you excited and itching to turn the page, here's a tiny taster of some of the fantastic skills I'm about to teach you:

- **How to make your opponent's ball find the water – every time**

- **What to wear to distract your opponent without getting thrown off the course**

- **When to unwrap your sandwiches* for maximum psychological impact**

- **Where to hold the pin when your opponent is putting**

There are no guarantees in life, but this isn't life, it's golf (although the two are remarkably similar – another point I make in this book), and I guarantee you that if your game doesn't improve after reading this book, not even for one brief moment, I will personally give you your money back.

Now, shall we play? My honour, I believe.

* NOT TO BE CONFUSED WITH SAND WEDGES. THAT'S A DIFFERENT CHAPTER ALTOGETHER.

# CAN YOUR NAME HELP YOUR GAME?

Golf used to be a sensible game for people with sensible names. Names like Colin, Nick, Ernie, Tom, Jack, Ian, Phil and Severiano. Then along came Tiger Woods and changed all that. He didn't just make golfers like you and me look ordinary, he made our names look ordinary too. (Well, our first names; he hardly went out on a limb with the Woods bit, did he?)

Such is the psychological frailty of the average golfer that games can be won and lost in the way you put your name down on the competitions board. You might see you've been drawn against someone called Tiger and your imagination starts to run away with you. 'Who is this Tiger? What does he look like? What if he's a real Tiger?' You've lost before you've even begun.

But let me say this right from the start:

> GIVING YOUR CHILD A FRIGHTENING NAME IS NO GUARANTEE THAT THEY WILL BECOME A CHAMPION GOLFER.

The bunker of golfing history is littered with supposedly intimidating names that came second best, or worse.

### FAMOUS LOSERS

**SHARK HUMPHREYS** – threw away a four-shot lead in the 1923 British Open

**MANTIS O'MARA** – involved in a record 47 play-offs and lost every one

**OSAMA JONES** – failed to make the cut at every Junior Masters since 2006

**VIPER JACKSON** – overlooked for Ryder Cup place five times in succession

**AK47 GREENBERG** – disqualified from The Open for hitting spectator on practice ground

**BIRDFLU BROWN** – failed to win any prize money in 17 years as a pro

# THE LENGTHS GOLFERS GO TO...

## No.1 The Moon

The farthest anyone has gone for a game of golf is the Moon. In 1971, Apollo 14 commander Alan Shepard hit a couple of 6-irons for the camera, while his colleague Ed Mitchell looked on. What we didn't see was that after the camera was turned off Shepard insisted on playing the entire course, with Mitchell carrying his clubs.

There's no shortage of holes on the Moon, or indeed bunkers, which makes it a tricky course in the best of conditions. That said, the lack of trees, water or wind is a bonus for the erratic golfer. The biggest challenge for the pro is getting your ball to sit down.

Shepard, normally a single-figures handicapper, went round in 364 that day and lost 28 balls, one of which caused panic in 1978 when it was spotted by amateur astronomer Steve 'Stumpy' Duckworth of Omaha, Nebraska, and falsely identified as an asteroid heading straight for Earth.

It has also been suggested that one of Jupiter's moons might actually be Shepard's tee shot at the 7th, which would make it the longest 3-iron in golfing history.

### THE GOLF GURU: 'YOUR PROBLEMS ARE MY GOOD FORTUNE'

**1. Fitness** Golfers have not always been considered athletes, but these days a healthy body is essential if you want to thrive in tournament golf. For sure, a tired body is a tired mind. When Jack Nicklaus came to me with short-game problems, the first thing I prescribed was a course of vigorous exercise in the gymnasium of my exclusive private clinic in Liechtenstein. The next week he won the US Open. Go figure. Put two golfers of identical ability head to head, the winner will be the one with the sweatier gym pants.

6

# THE ACTUAL HISTORY OF GOLF

## PART I Origin of the species

Golf, in one form or another, has been around ever since man first discovered the satisfaction of rolling round objects into holes. Stone Age golfer played with a pebble and the thighbone of a woolly mammoth, but bunkers were not part of the game, as anyone who went in one would have had to wait for the Iron Age before they could chip out.

# HOW TO BE A WINNER

## Arrive in style

No. 1

Here's a lesson I learnt the hard way. When drawn against an opponent who you haven't met before, first impressions can get you off to a flyer. The way you arrive at the clubhouse can make the difference between success and failure.

Anything with fewer than four wheels should be avoided, especially if the club has a gravel drive. There's nothing more counter-productive than coasting serenely into the driveway under the watchful eye of your opponent, wind in your hair and your clubs securely strapped behind you, and then skidding on the gravel and falling off your bicycle.

# DRESS TO DISTRESS

GOLF IS A PEACEFUL GAME –
NEVER BE LOUDER THAN YOUR TROUSERS

It's not essential to dress for golf, but it is expected of you. Ever since fearsome Jim MacDonald was disqualified from the 1691 Glencoe Open after being accused by his opponent of ungentlemanly conduct when he bent over to pick his ball out of the hole at the first, nudity has been frowned upon in championship golf.

You don't have to go to the same lengths as MacDonald to distract your opponent with your attire (or lack of it). The history of golf is bedecked with ingenious examples of off-putting fashion.

## ❶ The rabbit skin loincloth

Far more skimpy than the standard skins being worn at the time, the rabbit skin loincloth was the first item of fashion to really set golf apart from the high street.

## ❷ Plus fours

In an era of Corinthian values, sportsmanship in golf was assured by the arrival of plus fours, which made it very difficult for the cheat who liked to drop balls down the leg of his trousers.

## ❸ Rupert trousers

So named after the cartoon character Rupert Bear, who pioneered the look, Rupert trousers (pants, as some people call them) were *de rigueur* in the 1970s, along with Superman capes, Dennis the Menace shirts and Mickey Mouse ears.

## ❹ The patterned sweater

The hallucinogenic effect of diamond patterns was incorporated into the golfing jumpers of the late 20th century, giving the wearer the appearance of omnipresence and inducing dizziness in the observer.

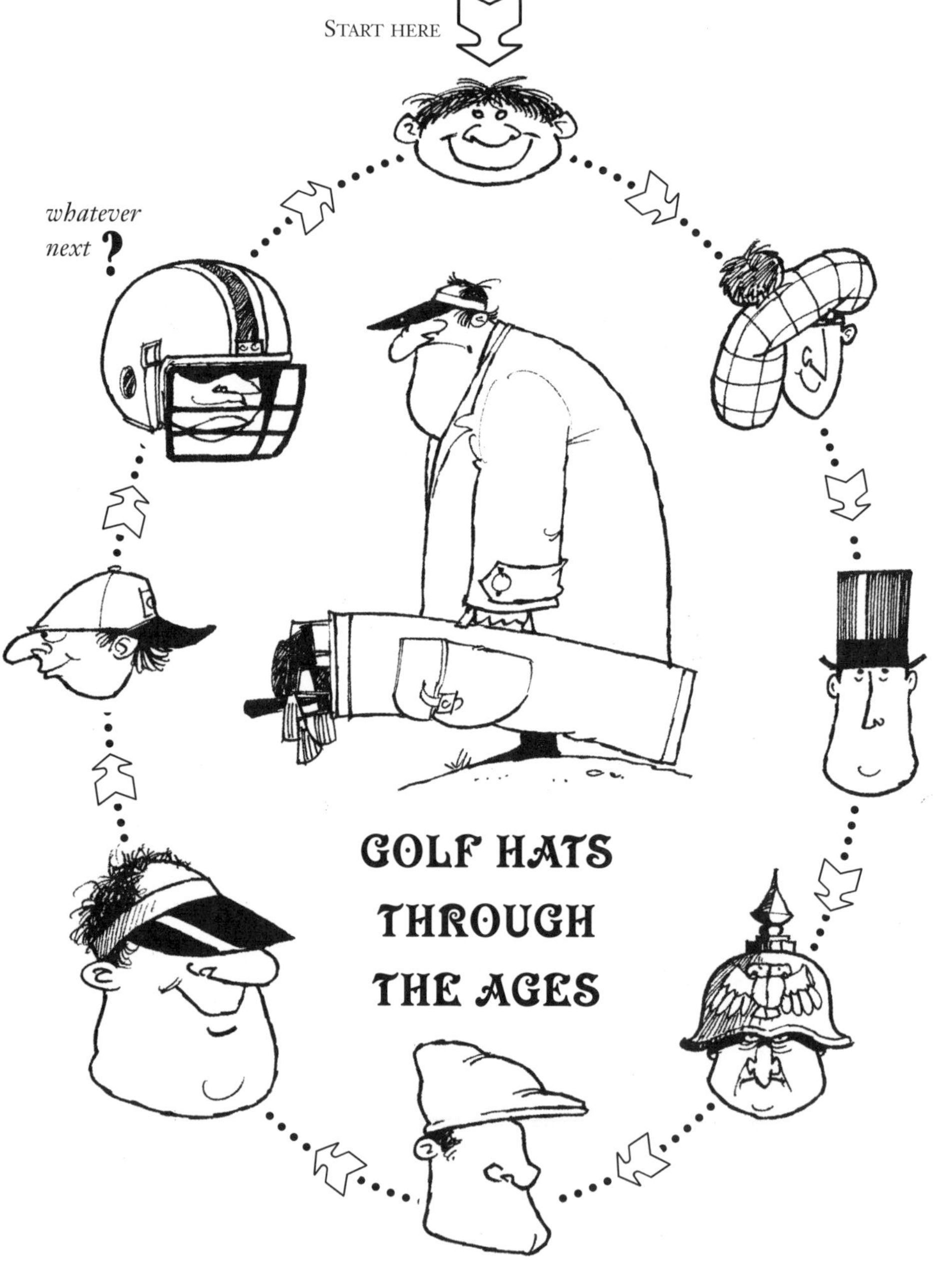
START HERE
whatever next ?
GOLF HATS
THROUGH
THE AGES

RECORD BREAKERS

## SHORTEST DRIVE

In 1975, Janice Goldsmith of Toronto, Canada hit a drive precisely nowhere. Yet it was not an airshot. In fact, she struck the ball cleanly but skied it straight up in the air. On returning to earth, it bounced twice and settled back on the tee peg.

# CHARACTERS TO AVOID

## No.1 The Club Captain

If you ever apply to join a proper golf club, you will be invited to play the Club Captain. There are two things you must remember:

1. DON'T PARK IN HIS PARKING SPACE
2. DON'T BEAT HIM.

You will recognize the Club Captain by his blazer and tie, and the other members genuflecting as he strides out to greet you. He is a powerful man. The president of the United States defers to his Club Captain.

His power is earned through hard work, vigilance and a willingness to do all the jobs that nobody else wants to do. The Club Captain is never off duty. If you're on the beach, he's the one wearing the blazer and Speedos.

### THE GOLF GURU: 'YOUR PROBLEMS ARE MY GOOD FORTUNE'

**2. Clean living** How you manage your affairs off the golf course has a terrific bearing on how you perform on it. Cleanliness and order, plus strenuous dental flossing at every available opportunity, will lead to more accurate putting as sure as night follows day. For sure, it's about tidying up after yourself, putting things away and keeping your environment under the strictest control. Run your finger along the shelves of any champion golfer's mansion and you won't find dust. Nick Faldo has trophies where lesser players have fluff. Fact. He never looked back after I instructed him to change his pants and socks every 18 holes.

# LEARN THE LINGO

Before you can cut a dash on the golf course, you have to learn the language. You wouldn't go to Italy without learning to say 'tutti frutti', would you? You'll hear a lot of strange words on the golf course, as well as a few familiar expressions used in unusual contexts. If you don't want to look an idiot, learn what they mean. Here's a quick quiz to test your knowledge.

**CHOOSE THE CORRECT MEANING OF EACH WORD FROM THE FOLLOWING OPTIONS:**

**BIRDIE**

**a)** A small bird
**b)** One under par
**c)** A shot that lands in a tree

**EAGLE**

**a)** A big bird
**b)** A shot that kills a rabbit
**c)** Two under par

**ALBATROSS**

**a)** Three under par
**b)** An even bigger bird
**c)** A shot played by mad sailors

**BOGEY**

**a)** Unwanted nasal produce
**b)** One over par
**c)** A swamp

**DIVOT**
**a)** A piece of turf cut up by the club
**b)** An underhit chip
**c)** A cross between a div and an idiot

**YIP**
**a)** Another word for yes
**b)** A loss of control of bodily functions when putting
**c)** A small tin for holding iron filings

**SHANK**
**a)** A mishit
**b)** A misfit
**c)** A leg of beef

**STYMIED**
**a)** Drunk
**b)** Piglike
**c)** Snookered

**DORMIE**
**a)** The feeling you get after spending too long in a dormitory
**b)** A lead that is equal to the number of holes remaining
**c)** A small mouse

**DOGLEG**
**a)** The leg of a dog
**b)** A Russian ballet dancer
**c)** A sharp bend in the fairway

*Answers on page 395*

Once you've learnt these words, start making up some of your own. You can really get under your opponent's skin with a few well-timed expressions designed to compound their insecurity.

**Wingle** a shot that just clears a water hazard, but then rolls slowly back into it.

e.g. 'Bad luck, old chap. You appear to have wingled.'

**Morfar** a putt that ends up further from the hole than where it started.

e.g. 'Hmm, that's an unfortunate morfar.'

**Cleeph** a drive which sends the tee peg farther than the ball.

e.g. 'Goodness! A cleeph!'

**Fantsie** a lucky shot that rebounds off a tree to the middle of the green.

e.g. 'Sorry, bit of a fantsie, I must confess.'

**Flump** a potential birdie that ends up two over par.

e.g. 'Never mind the flump, you played well up until the morfar.'

**Puldoon** an unspecified hazard.

e.g. 'Here we are: the 13th, with its notorious puldoon.'

A Cleeph

TIP

## THE YIPS

The Yips are caused by over-tension, brought about by standing too still over the ball. If you find yourself tensing up over your putts, try taking a run-up.

## KNOW YOUR GOLFING ETIQUETTE

**Q** *My tee shot has strayed from the fairway and landed on an adjacent green, where a four-ball are in the act of putting. How should I proceed?*

**A** Landing your ball on the wrong green while someone is trying to putt is a severe breach of golf's Code of Conduct, even though it is usually accidental. To avoid a dressing down, hide behind a tree until the four-ball have putted out. When the coast is clear, run out and chip your ball back on to the correct fairway, remembering to replace any divots. If the four-ball hang around waiting for you to show yourself, come out from your hiding place and walk very slowly towards them with a pronounced limp. Chances are they won't want to wait for you to get there and will move on.

# GOLF GADGETS

## No.1 The Umbrella

Apart from English bank managers, Mary Poppins and The Penguin, golfers are the only people who carry an umbrella at all times. A golf umbrella has to be bigger than any other umbrella. No one knows why. But there it is, it's a fact. If they started making normal umbrellas 10 feet in diameter, golf umbrellas would have to be 20 feet.

Golf umbrellas also differ from normal umbrellas in that they keep you dry. Their size may have some bearing on this. However, golfers do get wet, but from the feet up.

# MY GOLF NIGHTMARE

I have this recurring nightmare. I am a famous golfer and I am standing on the first tee at Augusta, about to play in the Masters. It's a lovely spring day, the sun is shining, the birds are singing in the trees and a large crowd has gathered to watch me tee off. The MC comes on the mic to announce my arrival on the tee ... and suddenly I realize I'm not a famous golfer, I'm Barty Thickett.

I've got my driver out by now and I'm standing over my ball trying to clear my head, but all I can think is

> WhatAmIDoingHere?Where'sTheHole?
> OhMyGod!HowAmISupposedToReach
> That?HowDoYouHoldThisThingAgain?
> Golly!ThatBallLooksSmall!WhyAreThey
> AllStandingInFrontOfMe?Shouldn't
> SomeoneTellThemToMoveBack...

CRACK. Before I know it I've played my shot. A voice behind me shouts,

> ***'IT'S IN THE HOLE!'***

And another yells,

> ***'YOU DA MAN!'***

And a third cries,

> ***'OH DEAR, I THINK HE'S HIT SOMEONE!'***

And there's a deathly silence and everyone turns to stare at me as if it's my fault, when we all know it's dangerous to stand in front of a golfer when he's about to play, and now someone's paid the price and bang goes my chance of winning the Masters.

I run to the spot where my ball struck and there's a man about my age lying prostrate on the ground, with my ball clenched between his teeth. On closer inspection I realize that it's me: I'm the person in the crowd who was hit by my own wayward drive. Me of all people – surely I should have known better. Now the competition referee's arrived and he's telling me I can take a drop for a two-shot penalty or play it as it lies. So I turn to my caddie and ask for a 3-iron.

Suddenly I'm the other me, lying on the ground looking up at me about to take a 3-iron and play the ball out of my own mouth. And I know what I'm like with a 3-iron, but I daren't open my mouth to scream because I'm afraid I'll swallow the ball…

And that's when I wake up. Apparently it's quite a common dream amongst golfers.

# CHARACTERS TO AVOID

## No.2 The Novice

You can spot a novice a mile off. Firstly, he or she won't be dressed to blend in. Brand-new clothes are the giveaway. He will also be trying to hide the fact that he doesn't have proper golf shoes yet. Then there's the walk. The Novice stalks about the course like an infantryman caught in open country, semi-crouching, constantly looking about for signs of enemy fire, ready to hit the deck at a moment's notice. He will also be zigzagging from one side of the fairway to the other.

Before you spot the Novice, you will probably hear him. Whoosh. Whoosh. The Novice seems to think you take your practice swing after addressing the ball. You'll also hear him saying things like, 'Why can't my grass look like this?' and 'Where's the pin?'

You might think winning against a Novice would be as easy as taking candy from a baby, but they have an irritating habit of absorbing all your advice and using it to good effect, without having the first idea how they did it. Then there's beginners' luck. Throw in that huge handicap and you're really on a hiding to nothing. If you do get drawn against the Novice, offer to swap partners with the Cheat (see The Cheat, page 100).

# THE SWING DOCTOR

## Your expert golf consultant

At its best, the golfer's swing can be a thing of rare beauty: a fluid, apparently effortless dance of limbs, torso and head in perfect harmony; an unhurried expression of the human form at the peak of its dynamic potential; languid, mellifluous, displaying all the natural elegance of a swan taking flight.

At its worst, it is a rather upsetting spectacle. I was once asked for advice by a man whose practice swing went so violently against the laws of nature that I assumed he needed medical assistance. By the time he came to address the ball I was on the phone to the emergency services, and he blamed my cry of 'Ambulance!' for his tee shot shying off at right angles into the woods.

Like most aspects of golf, there are countless things that can go wrong with your swing. Flat feet, crooked knees, rigid torso, wonky shoulders, arms… The arms regard the swing like the FBI regard a hostage situation. Never mind that your feet were first on the scene, the arms think it's all about them. It's their show now; they're in charge. Stand up to them and make sure the rest of your body gets involved. Remember, it's not just your arms that have to go looking for it.

Similarly, you would improve your swing no end if you removed your head. Your head is the control room and, as such, it clearly thinks it should play a bigger part than just sitting still on your shoulders and keeping quiet. Just when you want it to send a few useful reminders to your arms and legs, it starts thinking about donuts or childbirth or, worst of all, what would happen if you screwed up this shot and sent the ball deep into the trees.

And try as you might to keep it still, it just can't help looking up just before you make contact, so it can be first to see where the ball goes.

DON'T LOSE YOUR HEAD – JUST PRETEND IT'S NOT THERE

## WHERE IT CAN ALL GO WRONG

An anatomical study of the golf swing.

**Fingers:** For gripping the club. Interlocking right small finger with left index finger will also help you get your son a place at private school.

**Wrists:** Perform several functions at once, which can often prove too much for them.

**Head:** Imagine it's tied to the ball by a taut piece of string. (Lose this thought once the ball has been struck or you may involuntarily levitate.)

**Elbows:** A loophole in the central nervous system – trying to control them will throw you off balance and could cause incontinence.

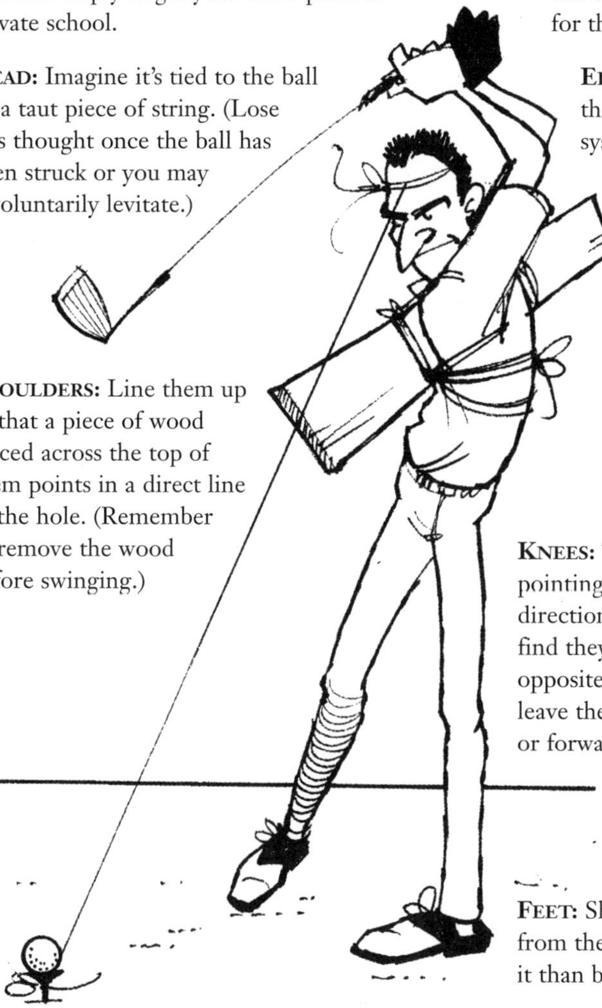

**Shoulders:** Line them up so that a piece of wood placed across the top of them points in a direct line to the hole. (Remember to remove the wood before swinging.)

**Torso:** Think of it as a coiled spring – but be careful not to overwind.

**Knees:** Try to keep them pointing in the same direction as your feet. If you find they're pointing in the opposite direction, quietly leave the course. Backwards or forwards, it doesn't matter.

**Feet:** Should be further from the ball after you've hit it than before.

# BLACK CATS AND FOUR-LEAF CLOVERS

Superstition is rife amongst golfers. You might be familiar with some of the following old wives' tales.

## It's a bad omen if...

☹ A black cat crosses your path just as you're about to drive.

☹ Your ball jumps out of the hole, followed by a toad.

☹ Your caddie hands you a ladder.

☹ You break the mirror on your golf buggy. (What are you doing with a mirror on your buggy anyway, you narcissist?)

☹ A sparrow lands on your head.

☹ An owl flies towards you with your ball in its beak.

## It's a good omen if...

☺ An owl flies away from you with your ball in its beak.

☺ Your opponent's ball knocks on wood.

☺ You find your ball on a four-leaf clover.

☺ You find a rabbit's foot by your ball. (Unless it's attached to a rabbit in a rabbit hole.)

☺ The bunkers form a horsehoe with the open end facing your way.

☺ Your jumper's on inside out (nobody will know the difference).

### COMMON GOLFING RITUALS FOR BRINGING GOOD LUCK

- Tuck your trousers into your socks.
- Wear your cap backwards.
- Leave your 1-iron in the clubhouse.
- Make sure your trousers and jumper don't match.
- Carry an eraser.
- Don't open your hip flask until the 7th.

# HOME PRACTICE

As a famous player once said to me, to be truly great at golf you have to apply the four Ps:

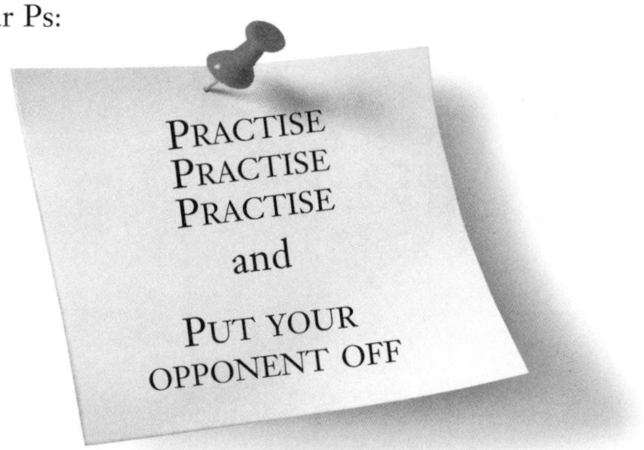
PRACTISE
PRACTISE
PRACTISE
and
PUT YOUR
OPPONENT OFF

Let's start with the first: Practise. You should practise every day, but it's not always possible to get out on the golf course every day, especially if you live in Japan. This is where home practice comes in. You can practise any part of your game in the comfort of your own home. All you need is a few props.

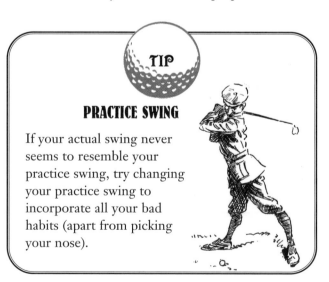

TIP

**PRACTICE SWING**

If your actual swing never seems to resemble your practice swing, try changing your practice swing to incorporate all your bad habits (apart from picking your nose).

# 1 Driving practice

**YOU WILL NEED:**

A large amount of plasticine

A bed sheet, preferably with floral pattern or other natural theme

14 wire coat hangers

A TV stand

Industrial strength glue

Roll the plasticine out to form a mat, about 10 feet by 5 feet and one inch thick. Unwind the coat hangers and join them together to form a large frame, about 6 feet square. Fix the bed sheet to the frame (you might wish to dye it so it resembles your favourite course, in which case the green half is at the bottom and the blue half is at the top). If you're feeling artistic you may wish to draw a distant flag in the middle of the sheet, or add bunkers. Place the entire frame and sheet on the TV stand at the far end of your plasticine mat (remove the television first) and fix it in place with the glue. Hey presto! Your own indoor driving range.

## 2 Bunker practice

**YOU WILL NEED:**

A corner bath

Some sand

A few cushions

Industrial-strength glue

A large laundry basket

Place the corner bath in one corner of the room (leave it where it is if you already have one in your bathroom). Fill it with about three inches of sand. Place the laundry basket in the opposite corner of the room. Glue cushions to the ceiling in a line between the bath and the basket. Practise chipping out of the bath/bunker into the basket. The cushions will protect the ceiling from over-enthusiastic bunker shots.

## ❸ Putting practice

**YOU WILL NEED:**

A carpet

Golf books

A large drill

A shell casing

A fencing sword with circular guard

Roll up the carpet and scatter the golf books randomly over the bare floor (any golf books will do, except this one, of course). Replace the carpet. Drill a hole 4.25 inches in diameter through the carpet and into the floor. Insert shell casing in the hole (if you can't get your hands on a shell casing, you can use the barrel of an old hand-held rocket launcher, cut down to size). Insert sword, handle first, into casing. You now have a green (or a purple, or whatever, depending on the colour of your carpet), complete with contours and one of those pins that lifts your ball out for you.

# GOLF GADGETS

## No.2 The Golf Bag

The primary purpose of the golf bag is for carrying that enormous umbrella. It also, cleverly, has space for your clubs, balls, gloves, waterproofs, tees and markers, sandwiches, drinks, shoes, socks, underpants, wallet, toilet roll and a small pencil.

Most of the pockets on your golf bag are obviously designed to hold specific parts of your equipment. There's a small one for tees, pencils, markers, etc., and a medium-size, quite deep one that's clearly for balls. There'll be an elasticated netting bit which is handy for your glove or scorecard. And then there's the long pocket: what's that for? It's not long enough for any clubs or umbrellas; it's too long for any item of clothing. The long pocket is every golfer's opportunity to show their individuality.

**THINGS YOU COULD KEEP IN YOUR LONG POCKET**

Telescope

Baguette

German sausage (large)

AK47 assault rifle

Fold-up stool

Crowbar

Wrapping paper (rolled)

Snake (dead)

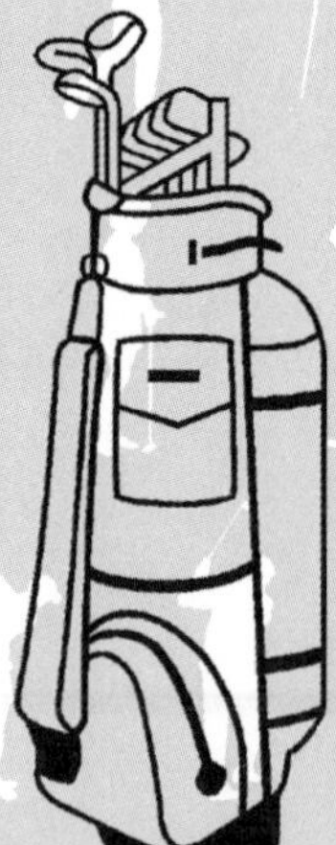

Although it's tempting to fill all those pockets, try to stop short of the full drinks cabinet, as weight can be a handicap. This isn't horse-racing! It also makes it hard to find things in a hurry.

# THE ACTUAL HISTORY OF GOLF

## PART II

## Flying Dutchmen

The Dutch invented a game that sounded a bit like 'golf' if pronounced with a thick guttural accent while sneezing, but involved several players all trying to hit one ball at the same time. The game's chaotic nature appealed to the French, who taught it to some Scottish soldiers during a lull in the Hundred Years War.

# MEDIEVAL INSTRUMENTS OF TORTURE

Several centuries ago, during the ban on golf, club makers had to find other outlets for their skills. The obvious market was the torture business, which was thriving, and golf clubs joined the many other cruel and sadistic devices widely used throughout Europe for extracting confessions.

**INSTRUMENTS OF TORTURE**

Iron maiden

The rack

Thumbscrew

Sand wedge

# GOLFING AILMENTS

All but the very best golfers are usually carrying at least one of these common ailments at any given moment. Don't worry. It will pass in time… and be replaced by a different one.

## Hook

## Slice

# Shank

# Air shot

# Yips

# CHARACTERS TO AVOID

## No.3 The Stickler (aka the Knowall)

There are many rules governing the game of golf, most of which you can disregard… until you come up against the Stickler. Sometimes it's interesting to know how the rulebook deals with certain unusual situations: e.g. does a King Cobra lying within striking distance of your ball count as a 'loose impediment'? But the Stickler isn't interested in this kind of fun. The Stickler is the only player who actually carries a copy of the rulebook, and the only reason he does is so he can spoil your fun.

Whatever magnificent acts of golfing heroism you may perform, the Stickler will find a reason to burst your bubble with some niggling little rule that forces you to walk the 350 yards to retrieve that magnificent drive, walk all the way back and hit it again, no doubt straight into a bunker this time, and suffering a one-stroke penalty for your trouble.

**NB:** The Stickler and the Cheat are often one and the same. Don't be fooled.

# THE MOST DANGEROUS SHOT IN GOLF

We've talked about all the various mishits, but there's one shot you should watch out for above all others, and that's the pearler.

The pearler is the shot you catch clean, the one you time to perfection, that leaves your club with barely a murmur and sails away, straight as a die, right where you aimed it. Arnold Palmer couldn't have hit it better. And when it lands you realize with swelling pride that you judged the distance just right. It bounces once with a little bit of bite, bounces twice, then settles down and rolls towards the pin, coming to rest a cool 18 inches short, and a voice in your head screams,

I CAN PLAY
THIS GAME!

Your opponent gives you the putt from 200 yards away and you march down to the green wearing a grin the size of Luxembourg, whistling a tune from *Oklahoma* and waving to the birds that seem to be applauding you from the trees.

Sounds like a dream shot, doesn't it? So why should you be wary of it?

Because the pearler is the shot that keeps you coming back for more. It is the baby's cry amidst the agonies of childbirth, the moment that sticks in the mind while all the pain is erased from memory. You may not play another shot like it for the rest of your life, yet it will always be with you, somewhere in the back of your mind, reminding you, 'You can play this game. You've done it before, you can do it again.'

So if you're just planning to be a casual golfer, playing every once in a while, not really intending to take it seriously, beware the pearler. Once you've played it, there is no escape. You will never play a 'casual' game of golf again.

## KNOW YOUR GOLFING ETIQUETTE

**Q** *I am playing against a lady who has mastered the art of breaking wind just as I am about to play my shot. Would it be deemed unchivalrous to confront her on this blatant act of gamesmanship?*

**A** Absolutely! This may be the 21st century, but I don't remember hearing that it had become acceptable to draw attention to a lady's flatulence, whether in the sporting arena or not. I'm afraid you find yourself in a position where the only course of action is to grit your teeth and play through it.

# RECORD BREAKERS

## WORST PUTT

Rick Plumstoner, a taxi driver from Woomera, Australia, hit a three-foot putt that ended up a thousand miles past the hole. Plumstoner's putt missed the hole by half an inch but rolled off the green and down a concrete path towards the railway line, where it bounced on to the 8.47 Trans-Australian freight train and ended up in the sidings at Kalgoorlie.

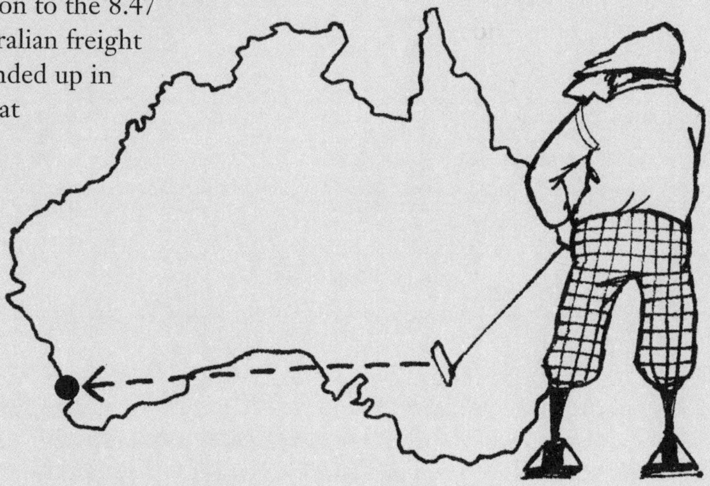

## TIP

## BOGEY CLUBS

If you have a particular wood that you never feel confident about using, swap your club covers around so your subconscious mind thinks you're using a different wood.

# HOW TO BE A WINNER

## Pick your competitions

**No. 2**

You can't win them all, so make sure you focus your efforts on the competitions that matter. How do you decide which ones count? Easy, take a look at the prize table. For instance, here's what was up for grabs at the last competition I played in.

- **A cut glass flower vase**
- **A bottle of Scotch**
- **A glove**
- **Some balls**
- **A large home-made pie**
- **2 tickets to the local production of *Oklahoma***
- **A cheese grater**

I came third and enjoyed a very pleasant evening with the Lady Captain courtesy of the local amateur dramatic society. But if you don't like Rodgers and Hammerstein, or flowers or Scotch, you don't fancy eating the same pie all week and you've already got a glove and plenty of balls, you might decide it's not worth playing your best golf for a cheese grater. It's a matter of personal taste.

# THE LENGTHS GOLFERS GO TO...

## No.2 Boston to Lexington at midnight

April 18th, 1775 is a famous date in American history. That was the night that Patriots Paul Revere and William Dawes embarked on a frenetic, hour-long horse ride from Boston to Lexington to arrive in time for an early-morning four-ball with John Hancock and Samuel Adams.

Revere had made his own set of irons and was desperate to try them out before being waylaid by the War of Independence. Hancock and Adams were two of the most influential players on the American Revolutionary circuit and Revere knew that if he and Dawes could impress them, his reputation would be guaranteed.

Little is known of the game itself. In his famous poem 'Paul Revere's Ride', Henry Longfellow fails to mention Dawes' miraculous bunker shot at the third, or Hancock's eagle putt on the 12th. Nor can we be sure who were the eventual victors when the four men shook hands on the 18th and Revere, suddenly appearing to remember something of importance that he was supposed to do, turned to his opponents and said, 'Oh, by the way, the British are coming.'

18

# THE ACTUAL HISTORY OF GOLF

## PART III A farewell to dung

The Scots refined the game into golf as we know it today, although they denied any Dutch involvement, claiming it evolved from the ancient Gaelic pastime of tapping deer droppings into rabbit holes with an inverted shepherd's crook. Golf, as they renamed it, proved hugely popular and was promptly banned.

### THE GOLF GURU: 'YOUR PROBLEMS ARE MY GOOD FORTUNE'

**3. Diet** You've heard the expression 'you are what you eat', yes? Then why do you eat so much deep-fried *Gelumpe*? Put your life under the microscope: is there balance in what you stuff inside yourself? Not forgetting, you must eat small to win big. No wonder you're so full of self-doubt and self-loathing whenever you try to wield a 3-iron; you're probably visualizing the contents of your stomach. Yeuch! But don't despair, we are all friends here; it's nothing a couple of coffee enemas can't solve. If it worked for John Daly, it'll work for you. Believe me, I was the one holding that bucket. I'll never drink cappuccino again.

# WHY GOLFERS GET SO ANGRY

People get annoyed on golf courses. That's an understatement, of course. In fact, they get so riled that they will take a brand-new club, which they've just spent a week's wages on, thinking it will be the answer to all their problems, and they will bend it over their knee, wrap it round an innocent tree (if any tree on a golf course could be deemed innocent), or fling it into a lake, to watch it sink like Excalibur, along with their hopes of a decent round.

The one sport that rivals golf for anger inducement is hockey, and guess what, it involves hitting a small object with a long stick. It's a phenomenon that can be explained very simply by Thickett's Law of Irritating Sports, which states:

> 'THE POTENTIAL OF ANY SPORT FOR RENDERING ITS PARTICIPANTS IRATE IS INVERSELY PROPORTIONAL TO THE SIZE OF THE BALL AND EXPONENTIALLY PROPORTIONAL TO THE LENGTH OF THE STICK WITH WHICH THEY'RE SUPPOSED TO HIT IT.'

Or put another way:

$$L2 \text{ x } \frac{1}{B} = K$$

Where L is the length of the stick, B is the diameter of the ball and K is the likelihood of bending your equipment over your knee.

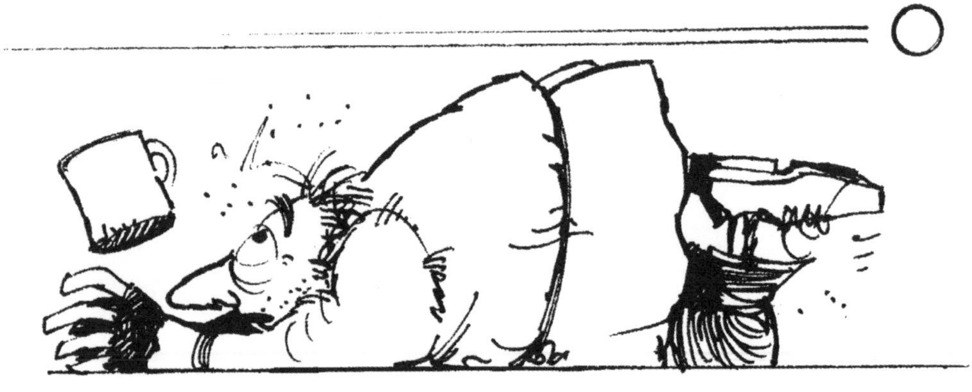

## DR PSYCHO EXPLAINS

The act of hitting any object with a stick takes us back to primeval times, when our ancestors enjoyed beating small animals with clubs in order to tenderize them before eating. The anger that accompanied the act was a chemical by-product that prevented prehistoric man from feeling too sorry for the small, fluffy animal he was bludgeoning. It also aided accuracy. This essential part of the process of survival has remained within the human psyche throughout evolution, and is most prominent in golfers and hockey players.

# IS IT LUCKY TO GET A HOLE IN ONE?

*I got a hole in one once and it cost me seventy-five big ones in the bar, so don't tell me it was lucky...*

*Mind you, I was only aiming to get on the green, and it skipped over a bunker on the way, so I guess it was a bit lucky...*

*But then what if my eye had registered where the pin was and the rest of my body had fallen into perfect alignment to strike the ball in exactly the right way to hole it? There's no luck in that, that's sporting perfection...*

*Unless you consider me lucky to have been blessed with a mind and body that is capable of perfection...*

*But I could have chosen to sit at home and watch Dukes of Hazzard videos, instead of taking the initiative to go out and play; so you could say I made my own luck...*

*But then I seem to recall that my TV was broken that day, so fate may have played a part...*

**Conclusion:** If you want to get a hole in one, break your television.

TIP

## STRAPPED FOR CASH

If you hit a hole in one but can't afford to buy drinks all round in the bar, offer your playing partner two drinks to keep quiet about it.

## KNOW YOUR GOLFING ETIQUETTE

**Q** *I've packed some sandwiches and a chocolate bar in my golf bag, which I've saved until the 10th. However, my opponent has already eaten his snack during the outward nine (without offering me anything). Should I offer him a sandwich?*

**A** It depends on the score. If you are leading fairly comfortably, it could put the final nail into his coffin if you were gallant enough to share your snack with him. However, if it's finely balanced, this could be regarded as a sign of weakness. You are perfectly within your rights to keep your snack to yourself (as he did) and enjoy the psychological advantage you'll gain from forcing him to watch you eat. And with this in mind, it always pays to put some effort and imagination into making your sandwiches. If your opponent sees you've overlooked the mayonnaise, for example, it could swing the initiative back his way.

# GOLF GADGETS

## No.3 The Stickwithgolfballpickerupper

One way in which golf suffers by comparison to other sports is the scoring. I don't mean the adding up of everyone's scores, I mean the actual physical act of holing out. In tennis, your opponent hits the ball in the net and a child runs and picks it up. In soccer you kick it in the net and their goalkeeper has to pick it out. In American football, you chuck the ball on the ground and the opposition have to go and get it. But in golf, you roll it down a hole and then you have to bend right down and pick it out again. It would all be so awkward and undignified if some clever golfer hadn't thought to invent the stickwithgolfballpickerupper.

# CHOOSING A CADDIE

Golf is the only sport I can think of where people offer to carry your equipment when you turn up to play. You don't get that in darts. Or Greco-Roman wrestling.

The word 'caddie' comes from the French for a sullen young boy who has been kicked out of the house to earn some pocket money, although these days your caddie is just as likely to be a girl.

Choose carefully. Don't just pick the first one you see. Caddies come in all shapes and sizes and you should base your choice on the same criteria as you would base your choice of car.

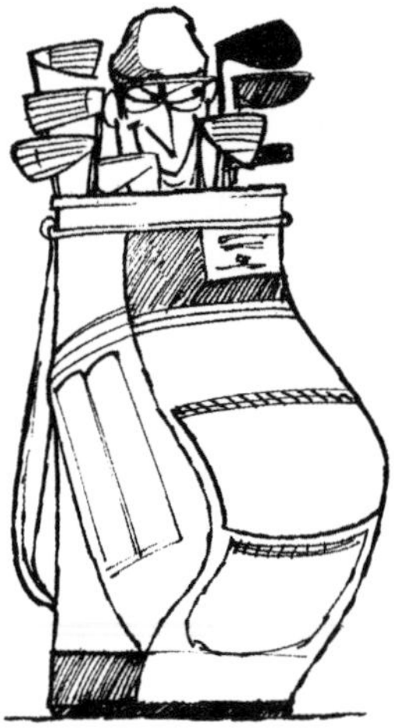

1. Make sure they're not older than you are.
2. Do they look like they've got several miles in them?
3. What's their carrying capacity?
4. Do they make any annoying noises?
5. How much is the asking price?
6. Do they have any sell-on value?

That last one might not apply in countries with strict labour laws.

# HOW TO BE A WINNER

## Visualize victory

No. 3

A good tip I learnt from Jack Nicklaus is to visualize yourself winning. Or was it Jean Van de Velde? I forget. Anyway, the point is if you can't see yourself winning, you never will. There are a number of common factors that undermine a golfer's confidence:

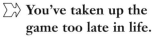

- **You've taken up the game too late in life.**
- **Your newest club was used as a weapon in the Crimean War.**
- **You're not very good.**
- **You should be at work.**

Just put these thoughts out of your mind. OK, so most top golfers took the game up when they were four, but it's never too late; just look at, erm... Clubs don't matter; it's the player that matters. And don't let that put you off either. Everyone was not very good once. And work can always wait. Just turn off your phone.

I tried this technique last time I entered a competition. I made myself comfortable, closed my eyes, breathed deeply, in through my nose, out through my mouth, relaxed my mind and began to see myself as a champion golfer. I drove the ball straight and true, I chipped with finesse and putted with unerring accuracy. Next thing I knew I was back in the clubhouse, feeling an amazing sensation I'd never felt before. I'd slept through the entire competition.

# FORGOTTEN CLUBS

I don't mean clubs as in the Potterton Thalmey Golf Club, where I first went round in father's buggy. Ah, I remember it well. Mrs Foldingbrass lecturing me for burping during her tee shot (I was only 2), then sending her approach shot into the ornamental pond after mistaking her niblick for her cleek. Happy days.

I mean clubs as in mashie niblick. Like the dodo, the mashie niblick is famous for no longer being in existence – a fine claim to fame if ever there was one. And just as the dodo is but one of a whole host of birds that have fallen permanently from their perch, the mashie niblick is just one club among dozens that once graced the golfer's armoury, but have since been lobbed into the woods forever.

**Feckle** a short-handled club with a pointed head, for scratching between the shoulder blades

**Squeezer** a rubber-shafted club with a hexagonal head, for taking pot luck.

**Gore's Bludgeon** a heavy club with a brick on one end and a head guard on the other, for playing out of dense forest.

**Teep** a lightweight club with a long shaft and tiny head, for lending.

**Muldenbaff** a forerunner of the modern driver, with a thick oak shaft attached to a cow's head.

**Dandling Hat** a cheeky club for placing over your ball when no-one's looking and moving it to a better lie.

**Piddling Cup** a long-handled club with a concave, perforated head for playing out of shallow water.

**Parcival's Shame** a low-profile club with a cushioned head, for playing quietly out of the clubhouse bar.

# CHARACTERS TO AVOID

## No.4 The Dog Walker

There are certain people who believe that large open spaces of natural beauty aren't just for playing golf on – and most of these people own dogs. OK, so dogs have to be walked, and a bit of fresh air does us all good, but it strikes me as a very bad idea to walk a dog on a golf course, for several reasons:

1. EVERYONE KNOWS WHAT HAPPENS WHEN A DOG AND A BALL COME INTO CLOSE PROXIMITY.

2. DOGS DON'T UNDERSTAND THE WORD 'FORE!'

3. DOG WALKERS TEND TO FOCUS ON THEIR DOG, RATHER THAN THE BALL TRAVELLING AT 200MPH TOWARDS THEIR HEAD.

The trouble is, the Dog Walker seems to assume that the golfers on the course are in complete control of their ball. Perhaps they've only experienced top-class golf. Perhaps they think it's safe to stand a couple of yards from the line of fire, like they do on TV. But even those spectators don't turn their back on the ball!

The most annoying thing about the Dog Walker, though, is that they seem to think you're involving them in your game – as if you're just hitting your ball so their dog can chase it. And when it fetches it and brings it back to your feet, covered in slobber, they look at you as if they expect praise. The Dog Walker, I mean, not the dog.

# PLAY YOUR HOME TOWN

When my local course is waterlogged or I haven't got time to drive out of town, I like to keep my hand in with a round of Urban Golf. The main differences between Urban Golf and normal golf are that it's free, you can dress down and there are a few more people to hit. Consequently, it's popular among scruffy, cheapskate psychopaths. If that's not the mark of a great game, I'd like to know what is.

There are also some rules that you don't find in normal golf, e.g. you have to play around school playgrounds, not over them, and if you're playing through a shop, you must use your putter.

**A TYPICAL HOLE IN URBAN GOLF MIGHT LOOK SOMETHING LIKE THIS:**

- **Tee off from the top of the multi-storey car park by the shopping centre, aiming towards the post office which stands at the end of Churchill Avenue.**
- **At the roundabout, take the third exit into Roosevelt Road, keeping it straight between the school on the left and the Salvation Army drop-in centre on the right.**
- **Chip over Mrs Jones' house, cutting the corner into the park on Stalin Street (watch out for the duck pond and Mrs Jones' dog, not to mention Mrs Jones).**
- **Hole out against the door of the ladies' toilet.**

# THE ACTUAL HISTORY OF GOLF

## PART IV Royal and Ancient

Mary Queen of Scots became the first lady to break 100 at St Andrews, much to the annoyance of her cousin Elizabeth, who was still on the waiting list. Later, as the game caught on in England, Charles I became the first player to sack his caddie mid-round, sparking the English Civil War.

# GOLFERS AND GOLF BALLS

Dear Santa,

For Christmas I would really like:

A car
A yacht
Nice trousers
A computer
Chocolates
A dining table
Guitar lessons
Socks

By the way, hope you've had a good year.
I think I've been quite good.

Regards to Mrs Santa.

Barty

For the last six years, I've written the same letter to Santa, yet every year I've rushed to the tree on Christmas morning and found the same present waiting for me: golf balls.

> JUST BECAUSE I PLAY GOLF DOESN'T MEAN I NEED GOLF BALLS!

The trouble with having a favourite pastime like golf is that it makes other people think they don't have to use any imagination in buying you presents. If it's not balls, it's books. Over those six years I have amassed a total of 67 golf books, including five copies of *Lost Balls* and eight copies of *Golf for Dummies*. Are they trying to tell me something?

Let me make it clear: I don't read golf books, I write them. And I don't need golf balls because, like all golfers except the really lazy ones, I find as many as I lose.

### WHY GOLFERS DON'T NEED NEW BALLS

I have a ball in my bag that is older than I am. I've never had to use it because I've never run out. This is one of the great mathematical equations that govern the game. You could call it a theorem:

**The more likely you are to lose your ball**

**=**

**The more time you are likely to spend looking for it**

**=**

**The greater likelihood of finding other balls**

In other words, your chances of losing a ball are equal to your chances of finding one. Tiger Woods never finds balls. And I find lots.
We both end up with the same number of balls as we started with.

I wonder if Tiger gets balls for Christmas.

## Lost and found

The difference between me and Tiger is that I tend to end up with better balls than I started with. It's a great feeling to go into the woods in search of a gnarled old range ball with tooth marks in it, and come out clutching a shiny new Callaway that some flash Harry couldn't be bothered to look for. It can almost make up for going in the woods in the first place.

It's tempting to keep looking even after you've found your ball, just in case there's a beauty lying nearby. (It's amazing how, with all that space, golfers land their mishits so close to one another.) You can take this too far, especially when it comes to water. Yes, it's tantalizing to see all those gleaming white balls beneath the waters of the lake, but, like coins in a wishing well, it's not the done thing to pull on your frogman's outfit and fish them out. You'll hold up the game.

There's nothing more annoying than losing your ball in the rough. To my mind, that's not what the rough's for; it's there to make the ball hard to play, not to swallow it altogether. That's what the woods are for. But if you're playing one of those Scottish courses, where their idea of a rough is my idea of dense rain forest, you can roll a couple of feet off the fairway and that's it – you might as well have hit it into the grasslands of the Serengeti.

## Why balls get lost

### (or The great ball manufacturing conspiracy)

**Question:** If you can fit a SatNav to a car to prevent it getting lost, why can't you fit one to a golf ball?

- **Player hits ball in rough.**
- **Player can't find ball.**
- **Player takes out SatNav and scans for signal from ball.**
- **Transmitter inside ball sends signal to SatNav via satellite.**
- **Player follows directions on SatNav.**
- **Player finds ball.**

It ain't rocket science. Well, apart from the satellite bit.

I wrote to all the major ball-manufacturers asking why they hadn't made such a device, and one of them came back with a refreshingly honest answer. I was told that if they made a ball that never got lost, they'd only sell one per player.

*'But what about all the ones they'd get bought for Christmas?'* I asked.

They had no answer to that.

# RECORD BREAKERS

## MOST CLUBS

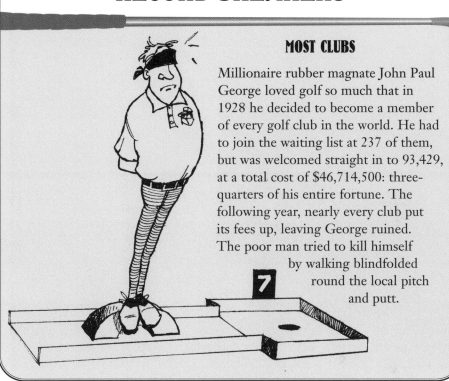

Millionaire rubber magnate John Paul George loved golf so much that in 1928 he decided to become a member of every golf club in the world. He had to join the waiting list at 237 of them, but was welcomed straight in to 93,429, at a total cost of $46,714,500: three-quarters of his entire fortune. The following year, nearly every club put its fees up, leaving George ruined. The poor man tried to kill himself by walking blindfolded round the local pitch and putt.

## TIP

### CORRECT A SLICE

A lot of players slice their drives. This is easy to correct. Just aim about 50 yards left of where you want the ball to end up.

# NEVER MIND THE WEATHER

Golfers are hardy souls. They won't let the weather spoil their fun.

❶ **Lightning**

## ❷ Hail

## ❸ Snow

## 4 Wind

# CHARACTERS TO AVOID

## No.5 The Liability

Everyone likes to make jokes at their own expense on the golf course. It's a way of lulling your opponent into a false sense of security. You'll hear a lot of people saying things like, 'I'm playing so badly at the moment, I'll probably miss the ball altogether and wrap my driver round my own neck.' The Liability is the one who means it.

When you play with the Liability you realize just how dangerous golf can be. These are the players for whom the word FORE! was invented. Don't just stand behind them while they're playing, stand behind a solid object, such as a tree or a brick wall. And never take your eyes off them, even on the green. X-ray departments in hospitals the world over are full of golfers who've made the mistake of bending over to pick up their ball before the Liability has putted out.

# A GOOD DRIVE SPOILED

If you fancy an easy round, try to get drawn against an older member of the club, preferably one who has difficulty walking. Hopefully they'll hire a buggy and you can cadge a lift. When a golfer gets to a certain age and their investments have done okay, they tend to join the ranks of the Regular Buggy Users (RBUs). Some will even have their own buggy garaged at the club, doubling up as a mobility scooter for doing the shopping.

The average age of RBUs varies greatly throughout the world. In Scotland, where masochism is part of the national identity, it is a matter of pride to carry your clubs at least until your 90th birthday. In the States, RBUs can start as young as 14 and you'll seldom see anyone over the age of 21 walking more than ten steps at a time, other than to relieve themselves in the bushes.

As golfers continue to hit the ball further, golf courses are going to get bigger and buggies are going to become an essential for every player. At the current rate of progress, by 2050 the average length of a golf course will be 150 miles. You'll struggle to get through 36 holes carrying your own bag. Even if you are Scottish.

The buggies of the future will have to be faster, more spacious and fully equipped for the futuristic golfer. They'll be powered by eco-fuels, of course, and will feature all the latest in-car entertainments.

## PIMP YOUR BUGGY

You don't have to wait to get more out of your golf cart. Here are just a few snazzy modifications you can make right now.

- **Fur-lined armchair seats for total comfort, with full race harness to hold you in when cornering**
- **Roll bar for extra safety on undulating courses**
- **Satellite dish, for in-car entertainment and SatNav ball tracking system**
- **Battery replaced with tractor engine powered by grass clippings**
- **Super wide wheels with low-profile tyres for soft ground**

- UV strip lights [underneath]
- Front mounted military grade searchlight for night golf
- Fully integrated sound system with twin turntables, MP3 and DVD player
- Wide-aspect plasma screen for watching movies and playbacks of your swing
- Top-of-the-range speaker system for precision sound reproduction between shots
- Small platform for caddie [on back]

## THE GRAVITATIONAL PULL OF WATER

Here's a conundrum that vexes the keen golfer: how is it that any small pond situated right in front of the tee will suck in golf balls like a black hole? Take the pond out of the equation and 99 times out of 100 your tee shot will travel at least 50 yards in the air.

Now introduce the pond and watch what happens. You will address the ball the same way that you always do, play your usual practice swing, clear your mind of all distractions, such as that small pond just in front of you... yes, that one... with the lily pads... that really small one that can't be more than 20 yards away and no more than 10 yards across... You pause at the top of your swing, keep your head stock still and your eyes fixed on the ball (forget about that pond), you swing, the ball flies off the club head and...

NOOOooooooooooooooooo. ***Plop!***

IT NOSEDIVES STRAIGHT IN AMONGST THE LILIES, AS IF THERE'S A MALEVOLENT NYMPH AT THE BOTTOM OF THE POND HOLDING A HUGE BALL MAGNET.

Similarly, if a course designer is careless enough to leave a lake down one side of the fairway, you are guaranteed to go in it. If it's on the left, a player who habitually slices will suddenly develop a hook. And vice versa if it's on the right.

A small watercourse running laterally across the fairway presents an intriguing dilemma: play safe and lay up, or go gung-ho and try to clear it. Don't waste too much time on this decision because either way you will end up in it.

And don't waste time trying to play it either.

A BALL LYING UNDER SIX FEET OF WATER IS **UNPLAYABLE!**

Such is the pull of water. Some people think it's purely psychological, but in fact it's all explained by physics. Sir Isaac Newton's law of universal gravitation states:

> ***'The force of attraction between two bodies is directly proportional to the product of their masses and inversely proportional to the square of the distance between them, and if one of the bodies is a body of water on a golf course, double it.'***

Which is why a golfer trying to play an awkward 8-iron while teetering on the edge of a lake is far more likely to fall in than fall out.

## PART V

## Higher, farther, wider

Great advances in technology brought a revolution in golf equipment. Beetroot was no longer used in the making of balls, and the lead shaft was replaced by hickory wood from America. As a result, standards and scores improved markedly, though it did take away some of the element of surprise.

# DRUGS IN GOLF

Along with things like club covers, pencil holders and a towel, one of the golfer's most valuable accessories is the hip flask. Golf is one of the few sports where you seem to improve with a drink inside you, although it's questionable whether that's because you actually start playing better or your maths just gets worse.

It's a very nerve-wracking sport and a little Dutch courage goes a long way. It's also nice to find a use for that hip flask your aunt bought you for Christmas when you told her you were sick of getting balls.

Apart from booze, though, I wouldn't bother with any performance-enhancing drugs. It's not like sprinting, where all you need is a drug that makes you quicker, or swimming, where you need something to help you float. For golf you need a drug that makes you aggressive then calm, powerful then delicate, happy then miserable... and so on.

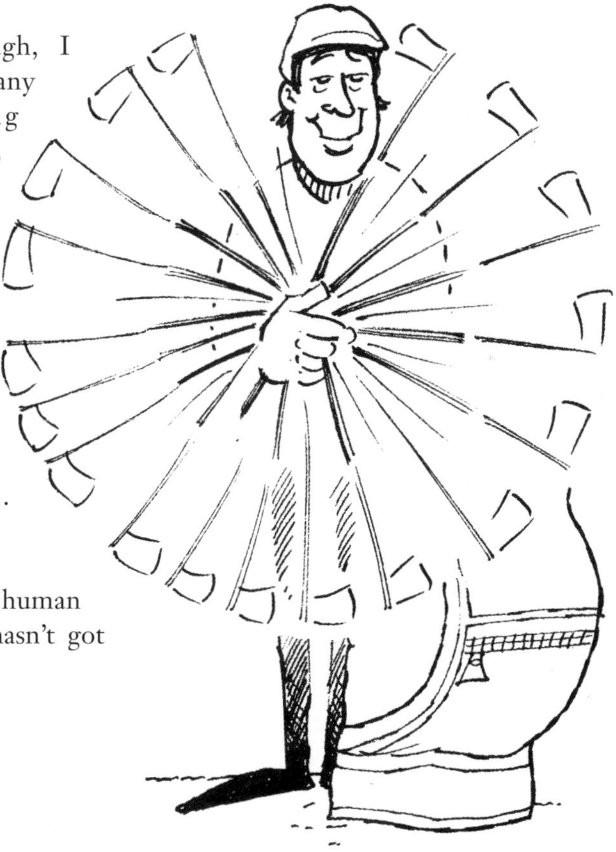

Some people have tried human growth hormones, but it hasn't got them anywhere.

# THE LENGTHS GOLFERS GO TO...

## No.3 Lake Tanganyika

Henry Stanley trekked for eight months through dense jungle to meet Dr David Livingstone for a round of golf at Lake Tanganyika Country Club in 1871. This was before they'd opened up the motorway. Unlike the moon, there are lots of trees and a vast body of water. Stanley lost four balls in the lake on the 6th.

Perhaps he should have given himself a couple of days to unwind after his long walk, but he was an impetuous adventurer and insisted on going out straight away. Greeting his opponent with the famous words, 'Doctor Livingstone, I presume we'll be playing off the white tees,' Stanley soon found himself sorely out of practice, and Livingstone, fresher and far more familiar with the course, having been there for a good five years, ended up winning 5 and 4.

*'Doctor Livingstone, I presume we'll be playing off the white tees.'*

# THE EFFECTIVENESS OF SHOUTING, 'FORE!'

The time has come to find a new word to replace 'FORE!' That's the conclusion of a recent study that looked at how people respond to having an old-fashioned word bellowed at them from a couple of hundred yards away.

It had been suggested that the word 'FORE!' was no longer fit for purpose, based on the alarming incidence of people being struck by golf balls (most of them dog walkers) despite receiving the traditional warning cry.

The researchers began by standing their sample group just to the side of the fairway, shouting 'FORE!' and measuring the response. The findings were as follows.

**Of the men**

**85%** showed no response.

**10%** ducked

**5%** shouted back 'five!'

**Of the women**

**75%** thought they were shouting 'fwoar!' and made a rude gesture

**15%** thought the same thing and waved

**7%** took cover

**3%** carried on talking

**CONCLUSION:** shouting 'FORE!' will only have the desired effect on average 8.5% of the time.

The same test was carried out using other old-fashioned words:

**GIMLET • HUZZAH • NARY • PRITHEE • WOAD**

The results were remarkably similar.

## WHY GOLFERS SHOUT

# *'FORE!'*

The cry of 'FORE!' originated as a variation of another four-letter Anglo-Saxonism, frequently used by 16th-century golfers whose shots went off course. Legend has it that it all began with Mary Queen of Scots, who forgot herself as she sliced a drive towards a group of courtiers on the 18th at Leith and shouted after the ball,

> 'FIE! FIE! FETCH YE HITHER YE WEE VILE CANKER-BOTTOMED APPLE JOHN YE. BY MY TROWTH WILL YE GET TO F…'

but caught herself at the last minute:

'…oooOORE!'

Her handmaidens, quick to spot the potential embarrassment, joined in the cry of 'FOOOOORE!' and kept shouting it until everybody was convinced that the queen had invented a new golfing expression.

# CHARACTERS TO AVOID

## No.6 The Cheat

Just as every village has its idiot, every golf club has its cheat. You can spot them quite easily, due to a number of telltale signs, e.g. they will always volunteer to play against the new member, who is guaranteed to be too naive or too polite to confront them.

When looking for their own ball, they always know to hunt on the edge of the rough, rather than deep in the trees where everyone else thinks it went. Yet they will find it, right there, in not such a bad lie after all. In fact, it couldn't be better positioned if they'd taken a new ball out of their pocket and placed it there.

They're also adept at playing out of bunkers, especially deep ones where you can't actually see them. They manage to dig the ball out with such control and accuracy, it's almost as if they've thrown it.

The Cheat is often a stickler for the rules (see The Stickler). It's the perfect smokescreen: they spend the whole round lecturing you on the finer points of the rulebook, and you don't notice that they've kicked their ball halfway round the course. At least, they think you don't.

TIP

## BEAT THE CHEAT

If you believe your opponent to be a cheat, wait until he hits a blind approach shot, then pick his ball up before he can find it and put it in the hole without him seeing. If he then claims to have found his ball on the edge of the green, he'll have some explaining to do when he holes out.

## KNOW YOUR GOLFING ETIQUETTE

**Q** *I have just holed out on the 18th and my opponent has a two-foot putt for a half. I detest the man. Should I give it to him?*

**A** Certainly not! A gimme is a golfer's way of saying, 'I like you.' Not giving a two-foot putt is a legitimate way of putting someone you despise through agony, without having to get him in a headlock. It is also an unspoken way of saying, 'You putt like a gorilla.'

# GOLF GADGETS

## No.4 The Ball Cleaner

Here and there on the golf course you will see a small wooden box with a handle sticking out of the side. This is for cleaning your ball. You put your ball in the machine, which also contains water and brushes, and you turn the handle vigorously until your ball is clean.

It's rare that you'll ever need to clean your ball, and yet it's impossible to resist – the ball cleaner is such a fun thing to use. The classic ball cleaner has given way to many weird and wonderful contraptions, but the fun never goes.

So much so that you find yourself looking for all sorts of other things to clean while you're at it.

# HAZARD COUNTY

The thing that makes golf unique is the variety of hazards you come across on the course. I often wonder how other sports might benefit from borrowing a few of these.

## Bunkers

# Deep rough

## Trees

# Gorse

# THE ART OF THROWING ONE

Giving vent to your feelings by throwing your club is an integral part of the game of golf and has been recognized as such since the early 1800s, when Scottish clansmen turned the practice into an organized event, as a forerunner to the Highland Games.

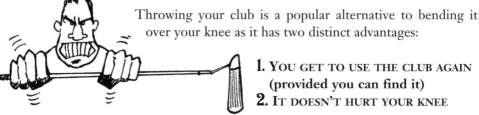

Throwing your club is a popular alternative to bending it over your knee as it has two distinct advantages:

1. **You get to use the club again (provided you can find it)**
2. **It doesn't hurt your knee**

The throwing technique differs little today from the one the Scots were using 200 years ago.

## 1 Pick your spot

Though it appears to be a spontaneous act, it's worth pausing for a second to consider the trajectory of your throw. This is a more recent refinement. Try to avoid hitting any bystanders and, if possible, throw it in the direction you're heading. Throwing it backwards or into the woods or water will only heighten your sense of indignation.

## 2 Backswing

Start by taking the club back as far behind you as possible, making sure to keep a firm grip. Forget the position of elbows, wrists, head, etc., just let nature take its course…

## ❸ Pivot

Don't just rely on your arms, use your whole torso and legs to spin round a couple of times…

## ❹ Release

On release, extend your arms in the direction you want the club to fly and let go at the last possible moment. If you've started shouting as you throw, bring it to a crescendo as the club leaves your hand.

# MATHEMATICS FOR GOLFERS

The scoring system for any sport varies in complexity according to the average trustworthiness of the people who play it. If soccer players could lie about the score they would, so it's scored very simply in ones. Rugby, on the other hand, attracts a more upright sort of character, and so is scored in a very complex way involving twos, threes and fives. And if you want someone to look after your kids for the weekend, ask a darts player.

Where golf fits in to this is ambiguous. In essence it has a very simple scoring system: every shot counts as one towards a grand total of all the shots taken. But the complexity arises when it comes to remembering how many shots have been taken, since they're not all noted down at the time. Therefore, the golfer has to carry a running total in his head, which isn't easy when you keep having to stop and hit the ball.

Here's a typical piece of mental arithmetic that golfers always find hard.

$1 + 1 + 1 + 1 + 1 + 2 = 7$ ➽ WRONG
*Correct answer* = 13

What the golfer tends to forget is that the first '1' was actually 3 off the tee; the 'second' (4) went into the water, requiring a drop (5); the 'third' (6) went into a bunker and took 2 to get out (8); the 'fifth' was preceded by an air shot (10); and it was three putts, not two (13).

So at the end of each hole comes the ritual 'counting back'. This is a process golfers go through in order to ensure their opponent isn't cheating, while appearing to be helping them out. The art is to run through their score in an inquiring tone of voice, as if you haven't been fastidiously counting every shot they took.

*'So you chipped out of the rough for two and then you hit your 7 iron into that nasty bush, didn't you, yes, so you had to take a drop, that was four, and then you played it back into the bush for five. Another drop for six, into the bunker, seven, deeper into the bunker, 8, in the bunker again, 9, finally out backwards for 10, on to the green, eleven, and three putts. Is that right?'*

*'Yes, that's right, thank you. Put me down for 14.'*

*'But you get a shot on this hole, so...'*

Thirteen it is, that last act of generosity lending the final touch to your insouciance.

However, an unscrupulous 'count backer' can use the same approach to enhance his own score. By being honest about the traps he fell into, a cheat can gloss over how many shots it took to get out.

*'I played my second into the bunker (actually it was your third), out to the edge of the green (it took you two goes), chipped on for four and one putt – five.'*

*'Wait a minute, didn't you take two to get out of the bunker?'*

*'Of course I did. I do apologize. So it's a six.'*

Actually, it's a seven, but he'll put down a five anyway, because by the end of the round nobody will be able to remember.

# SECRET ORDER OF THE HANDICAP

Not many golfers realize that they are espousing an ancient form of Socialism every time they play, and if they did, half of them would probably quit. I'm talking about the handicap system, the ingenious mathematical principle that enables the malco-ordinated 60-year-old to beat the finely honed 30-year-old.

The handicap system is golf's crowning glory, and it's based on a complex formula that no mathematician has been able to unravel, the secret of which is preserved and protected by a society of Handicappers, who meet in dark corners of independent bookshops every second Thursday of the month. Directly descended from the Knights Templar, their numbers are strictly limited and only when one Handicapper dies can a new one be created.

However, rumours of self-flagellation and the wearing of hair shirts and spiked undergarments are unfounded. The only masochistic ritual they observe is playing golf.

Most golfers don't even realize that the Order of Handicappers exists. They just hand in a card every so often and get given a figure. They don't stop to look twice at the person who's given it to them. And provided they keep it up to date, the Order never has cause to visit them. But woe betide the golfer who allows his handicap to lag, just to give him a better chance in competitions, for he shall be branded a BANDIT and will face the punishment dished out by the Order to those who presume to abuse its sacred code.

TIP

### DON'T GO EMPTY

Always carry some spare change in case there's a food kiosk halfway round the course. There's nothing more demoralizing than missing out on a bacon sandwich.

RECORD BREAKERS

### MOST ATTRACTIVE BODY OF WATER

Attractive to golf balls, that is. The Atlantic Ocean has consumed more golf balls than any other body of water, but pound for pound the most attractive water hazard ever recorded was a small pond in front of the 15th green at Sky View Golf Club, Michigan, from which local frogman Archibald Tent once retrieved 1,239 balls in just one week. In 1979 the pond was filled in and the clubhouse bulldozed by an irate member, who was later discovered to have been responsible for 1,200 of them.

# THE ACTUAL HISTORY OF GOLF

## Divots and diplomacy

## PART VI

During the Age of Discovery, golf spread throughout the world as an amusing distraction while discussing business or politics. Much of the world map was drawn up on the golf course, with whole countries changing hands on the 18th green, either lost in wagers or carelessly signed over while concentrating on a tricky three-foot putt for the match.

# HOW TO MAKE A REMOTE-CONTROLLED GOLF TROLLEY

There's something noble about carrying an enormous bag full of someone else's stuff for mile upon mile, looking interested, offering advice and getting abused, but as anyone who's watched *Tarzan* will know, there always comes a point at which your bag carrier refuses to go on and you're forced to carry your own gramophone player. (OK, so not many golfers carry a gramophone player – I'm talking metaphorically.)

Enter the Remote-controlled Trolley. This great gadget has two key selling points:

1. IT'S A TROLLEY
2. IT'S REMOTE-CONTROLLED.

But there are more advantages than that:

3. IT WILL IMPRESS YOUR OPPONENT
4. IT WILL DISTRACT YOUR OPPONENT
5. ESPECIALLY IF YOU KEEP MOVING IT WITH COMIC TIMING JUST AS THEY'RE ABOUT TO PLAY THEIR SHOT.

You can buy Remote-controlled Trolleys if you've got a spare grand in your back pocket, but if you haven't there's always the DIY approach. If you already have a trolley, it's easy to upgrade it into a Remote-controlled Trolley using everyday household items that you probably have lying around. If you don't already have a trolley, follow instruction 1.

**IN ADDITION, YOU WILL NEED:**

A rubber band

A cotton reel

A VCR

Remote control for the VCR

Industrial-strength glue

Batteries (AA and car)

**1.** Get a trolley.

**2.** Slide the axle of the trolley through the cotton reel and glue it in place. Loop the rubber band over the cotton reel and the other end over the spindles of the VCR (the bits that turn the tape). Glue the VCR to the trolley and connect up to the car battery. Glue the car battery to the VCR. Put the batteries in the remote control.

**3.** Press play to go. Fast forward to go faster. Stop to stop. Rewind to reverse.

**4.** For a steerable Remote-controlled Trolley you will need two VCRs and two cotton reels, one for each wheel. For in-trolley entertainment, add a third VCR and a TV screen.

# THE LENGTHS GOLFERS GO TO…

## No.4 The Antarctic

What began as an experiment in winter golf and a forerunner of the modern stag weekend turned into an epic tragedy when Robert Falcon Scott took his friends golfing at the South Pole. It was while looking for Captain Oates' ball after he hit a wayward 7-iron at the 14th that things went awry. The weather closed in and they were forced to abandon their round, with Norwegian rival Roald Amundsen already in the clubhouse.

Feeling guilty about spoiling everyone's trip, Oates announced that he was going back out to replay the shot, but was never seen again. In Scott's diary, which was discovered after his death, was a small footnote with the conclusion: 'A coloured ball, say luminous orange or green, would have made life easier.'

*'I'm just going outside…'*

# RECORD BREAKERS

## MOST HITS

Hitting another person with your ball is one of the worst feelings in golf, especially if it was on course for the green. On April 7, 1983, Brian Psaltipot (pronounced Salty-po) from Yorkshire, England, experienced that sickening feeling a record seven times in a club championship match.

He began by shanking a 5-iron across the 4th fairway and catching his opponent between the shoulder blades; he then misjudged a chip at the 5th and bent his caddie's nose; at the 8th he overshot the green with a 3-iron and hospitalized the greenkeeper, who was watching from his tractor; he followed this with the rare feat of hitting two people with one shot at the 13th, when his drive came down on the 14th tee, hitting one player on the foot and bouncing up into the other's chin; at the 16th, as if to make amends, he hit himself, crashing a 7-iron off a tree and catching his own shin with the rebound; and to round it all off, his approach shot to the 18th bounced off the path and straight into the midriff of his wife, who was waiting to see how he had got on. He came third.

# CHARACTERS TO AVOID

## No.7 The Hothead

This is a player you should avoid playing with, but jump at the chance of playing against. He will be a competent golfer, maybe even a great natural talent, and this will be his undoing. For the Hothead thinks he can do anything.

He will never lay up. He will always drive for the green on a par 5. He'll never play sideways out of the woods or rough, but will always go for the hole. And all obstacles are there to be outgunned. There's a 28-storey tower block between the tee and the green: the Hothead will try to drive over it.

If you're all square on the 18th tee, challenge him to a longest-drive competition. He won't be able to resist, and rather than playing the sensible shot to the middle of the fairway that will put you under pressure, he'll rip his ball into the woods, then do the same again with his third off the tee, leaving you the simple task of putting from tee to green for a match-winning 9.

### GOLF GURU: 'YOUR PROBLEMS ARE MY GOOD FORTUNE'

**4. Undergarments** A vest isn't just for cold days, it's for hot days too. For sure, it will add an extra layer of warmth when the air has a nasty nip, but just as important is to soak up all that glistening sweat in the lazy, hazy days of summer, to avoid catching a chill when the dampness cools, and to protect the extremities from chafing nylons. Many a pro has come to me with sore nipples on a summer's day and I've sent them away smiling, soothed by the comfort of a sensible cotton undergarment. You know, your mama had a tiny bit more sense than you ever gave her credit for. She teaches us to synthesize past and present for the best possible tomorrow.

# NOT QUITE GOLF

One of the great things about golf is that you can play any part of the game on its own and still have fun. You can't do that in soccer: imagine taking throw-ins over and over again. Or in tennis: who'd play a game that just involved hitting the ball into the net? But with golf, a bit like a restaurant that just serves pudding, you don't have to have the full meal, you can choose the course you like.

*'Too much bottom hand, George.'*

## ❶ Putting Green

**What is it?** A common sight in seaside towns, the putting green is where most small children get their first taste of golf. And their last.

**What's the point?** There are two schools of thought when it comes to the question of which is the most important shot in golf: some say it's the tee shot, others say it's the putt. In this respect, the putting green could be regarded as taking the essence of golf and distilling it to its purest form. Or you could just say it's golf for people who couldn't be bothered to walk very far or carry more than one club.

**Is it safe?** As all shots are relatively short and the ball does not travel in the air, it can certainly be classified as safe – unless your seaside resort happens to be downwind of a nuclear plant.

## ❷ Pitch and putt

**What is it?** Another popular attraction in holiday resorts, pitch and putt is where most kids learn about the dangers of golf.

**What's the point?** If the putting green is too one-dimensional, pitch and putt offers participants the challenge of getting the ball in the air first. It also teaches them about choice of club, and why you shouldn't try to hit the ball with two clubs at the same time.

**Is it safe?** No. The combination of novice golfers, lofted clubs and a small playing area is a recipe for disaster.

# ❸ Crazy golf

**What is it?** A popular seaside attraction (What is it about the seaside? Why don't people play these games in inner cities?), where young golfers first learn that life isn't fair.

**What's the point?** Crazy golf is an existentialist demonstration of the random nature of golf, showing, with the use of props, that you have as much chance of controlling where your ball ends up as you have of hitting it through the front door of a windmill while the sails are going round. Or something like that.

**Is it safe?** No. It's not the golf that's crazy, it's the people who play it that are driven crazy.

## ❹ Driving range

**What is it?** A place where you can practise any shot you like without worrying about where the ball goes.

**What's the point?** You can pretend you're playing an entire round of golf, but there's no walking involved and you never lose a ball. It's a bit like being a pro. There are usually some interesting targets to aim for, like a burnt-out car or an old phone box. You could be in Detroit. Sometimes they even send out a man on a tractor.

**Is it safe?** As long as you're not the man on the tractor.

### 5. Night golf

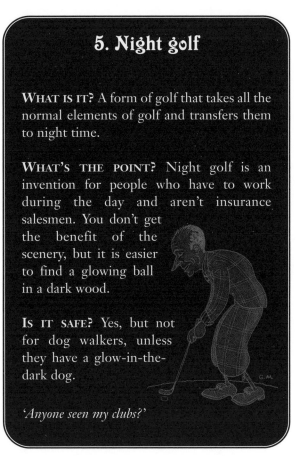

**What is it?** A form of golf that takes all the normal elements of golf and transfers them to night time.

**What's the point?** Night golf is an invention for people who have to work during the day and aren't insurance salesmen. You don't get the benefit of the scenery, but it is easier to find a glowing ball in a dark wood.

**Is it safe?** Yes, but not for dog walkers, unless they have a glow-in-the-dark dog.

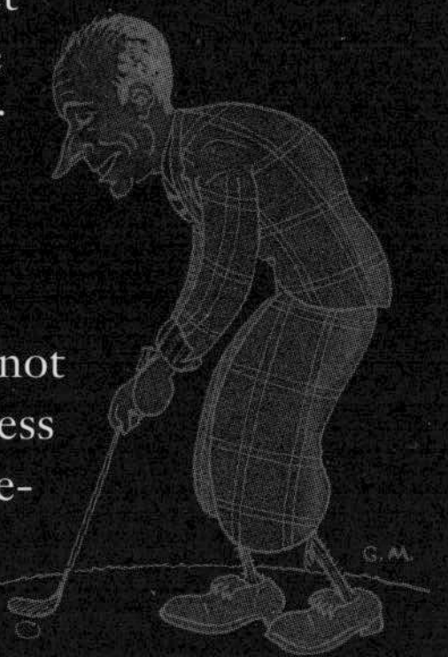


*'Anyone seen my clubs?'*

# PEOPLE WHO DON'T LIKE GOLF

Believe it or not, there are people who don't like golf. Most of them have never played the game, they just take an irrational dislike to people whose clothes don't match, or insurance salesmen, or people who still observe certain forms of segregation; some petty prejudice like that. But they don't admit that's their reason for disliking golf. They dress it up in some fancy language that makes them look witty.

***'A good walk spoiled.'*** **(Mark Twain)**

When did anyone ever go for a walk just for the sake of it? A good walk is one with a purpose, such as hitting a ball around with you and seeing how few times you have to hit it to make it go where you're walking. Therefore, a good walk spoiled would be a game of golf with the golf removed.

Mind you, Mark Twain was a river man, and his attraction to the water probably didn't help his golf.

***'An expensive way of playing marbles.'***
**(G.K. Chesterton)**

I don't know what sort of marbles you've been playing, G.K., or what sort of golf for that matter, but either way you've been getting it wrong. You might as well have said, 'An expensive way of playing cricket,' or 'An expensive way of playing billiards.' You were right about the expensive bit, though.

***'An arduous way to go for a walk. I prefer to take the dogs out.'*** **(Princess Anne)**

Hmm, been reading Mark Twain, ma'am? When was the last time you saw a golfer walking along behind his ball with a plastic bag and a trowel?

***'Golf appeals to the idiot in us and the child.'*** **(John Updike)**

Speak for yourself, Mr Updike. There's no child in me.

*'Golf is not a game, it's bondage.'* (JIM MURRAY)

I suggest you take another look at the rules, Jim. Someone's been having you on.

*'Like chasing a quinine pill around a cow pasture.'*
(WINSTON CHURCHILL)

You're trying too hard now, Winnie. We liked the 'Never in the field of human conflict' one and the 'We shall never surrender', but you lost it with this one.

*'A day spent in a round of strenuous idleness.'*
(WILLIAM WORDSWORTH)

Not sure what Will means, to be honest, but it sounds like a criticism. Note the use of the oxymoron, a common tactic used by poets to hide the fact that they don't know what they're talking about.

# GAMESMANSHIP

## or The art of arousing your opponent's inner demons

Not to be confused with cheating, gamesmanship is the practice of gaining maximum advantage over your opponent without straying outside the laws of the game. A lot of golfers frown on it. Well, they pretend they do.

Golf is a very simple game made vastly complicated by the human imagination. As an impassive bystander, you can look at a player's lie and their line to the pin and see that two simple shots will put them inches from the hole. But if you want to complicate things for them, offer them a helpful tip:

**'Mind that small pond on the left.'**

And then they've had it. Instead of standing over the ball thinking, 'Nice easy approach, two putts, par,' they're thinking,

'SMALL POND ON THE LEFT, SMALL POND ON THE LEFT, SMALL POND ON THE LEFT.'

And ***Splash!,***

in they'll go. It works every time. They hadn't even noticed the small pond on the left until you mentioned it.

The art of gamesmanship can be broken down into three basic disciplines:

### 1 The reality check

If the key to playing well is to clear your mind of all other distractions, your job is to put those distractions back into your opponent's mind. This is particularly effective on the first tee.

**YOU:** 'Your honour then.'
**OPPONENT:** *'Thank you.'*
**YOU:** 'Best of luck.'
**OPPONENT:** *'Kind of you.'*
**YOU:** 'Lovely day for it.'
**OPPONENT:** *'Isn't it just?'*
**YOU:** 'Quite a crowd on the balcony.'
**OPPONENT:** ***'Gulp.'***

Now how is that unsporting?

## ❷ The power of suggestion

Choice of club is a rich seam worth tapping. There are two ways of luring your opponent into making the wrong choice, the first being to throw down a very subtle gauntlet.

**YOU:** 'Is this your ball?'
**OPPONENT:** *'Ah yes, well found.'*
**YOU:** 'Bit of a tricky lie.'

**OPPONENT:** *'Hmm, yes, never landed in a tree before. I think I'll take a drop.'*
**YOU:** 'Very sensible. Mind you, I saw someone take a wood in a very similar position and put it three feet from the hole.'
**OPPONENT:** *'Really?'*
**YOU:** 'Really. But if you want to play safe…'

## ❸ Flattery will get you everywhere

The second way to delude your opponent into the wrong choice of club is to blind them with flattery.

**YOU:** 'What a magnificent drive.'
**OPPONENT:** *'Thank you.'*
**YOU:** 'Much further than mine.'
**OPPONENT:** *'I suppose I did catch it rather well.'*
**YOU:** 'Absolutely. Leaves you a nice easy wedge to the green.' (Ha! A 6-iron more like.)

# ❹ Noises off

Starting a conversation or singing during your opponent's backswing lacks the subtlety required of the high-class gamesman, as does 'accidentally' dropping your clubs. But there are other ways to distract your opponent with unwanted noises.

I once played against a judge and his wife, who, he confided to me during the round, was known affectionately as 'The Hand Grenade', due to her remarkable ability to break wind very loudly and at will. He also told me she had never lost a match on the 18th. When we came to the final green, I found out why. Faced with a relatively simple putt for a half, I was completely put off my stroke by the lady asking me quite nonchalantly if I'd like her to remove the pin.

# FAMOUS SONGS INSPIRED BY GOLF

**Stairway to Heaven** Began life as 'Fairway to Heaven', Robert Plant's tribute to the 6th on the New Course at Sunningdale.

**Tea for Two** Originally 'Tee for Two', this 1920s classic was conceived as a ditty about booking a round of golf.

**Shut Up and Drive** In Rihanna's hands this song evolved from a simple golf sentiment to a more streetwise motoring/sex metaphor.

**I Talk to the Trees** The wistful musings of a golfer looking for his ball, this became a surprise hit for Clint Eastwood in the film *Paint Your Wagon*.

**The River** Springsteen's original chorus, 'We'd go down to the river, and into the river we'd dive, cos into the river we'd drive', says it all about a pair of golfers finding the water.

**19** The original storyline, about a golfer who had developed a stammer from spending too long in the clubhouse bar, was deemed too near the knuckle, so it was changed to a lyric about Vietnam.

## RECORD BREAKERS

### DEEPEST DIVOT

In September 1992, a golfer trying out a new course in Dubai took a divot on the third fairway and struck oil. His stroke knocked the crust off a well that was lying very close to the surface. Geologists later estimated it to be 250 metres deep.

# GOLF GADGETS

## No. 5 The Rescue Club

In most cases the term 'rescue club' is a complete misnomer, implying that it can rescue you from any nasty situation and leave you in a great position. In most cases they just throw the ball up in the air and land it more or less back where you started. The exception is what I call 'the retriever'; a wire cup on the end of a telescopic pole, for fishing your ball out of ponds.

In skilful hands it will salvage any sunken ball and deliver it to dry land for the cost of just one shot, and it doesn't even count as a club, so you can still carry 14. I also find it comes in handy in the kitchen.

# THE ACTUAL HISTORY OF GOLF

## Let battle commence

## PART VII

The invention of the atom bomb finally rendered golf obsolete as a weapon of war. Up until then it had played a key role in many famous conflicts, including the Battle of Hastings (it wasn't an arrow that took Harold's eye out), Agincourt ('Once more unto the tee, dear friends!') and Little Bighorn (question marks remain over Custer's choice of club).

# CHARACTERS TO AVOID

## No.8 The Comedian

Go for a round of golf anywhere in the world and you'll be doing well not to come across a Comedian. I don't mean golfers who think they're funny, I mean people who make a living out of being funny yet seem to spend their daylight hours on the golf course. The world of showbiz is full of golfers, and always has been.

There are a number of professions that are drawn towards golf: salesmen, footballers, taxi drivers. It doesn't take a quantum physicist to work out why golf appeals to these guys. But why so many Comedians?

Here's my theory: Comedians play golf to have a break from laughter. When was the last time you saw someone play a duff shot and everyone else cracked up laughing? It doesn't happen.

### Golf isn't funny

Golf is the one area in life where a man getting covered in sand doesn't get a laugh.

But it all changes if the Comedian starts losing. When they feel the game is lost they start clowning around, pulling joke clubs out of their bag, hitting balls that explode on impact and generally making a mockery of the whole thing. It destroys any satisfaction you might get from beating them.

# LAST GASP

It is the ambition of many golfers to die on the course, if only so they can crack the old joke at the Pearly Gates.

**St Peter:** ***'What are you here for?'***
**Golfer:** ***'Three.'***

Golf is a game you can go on playing later in life than any other sport, so the chances of 'holing out' during a round are higher than average. It strikes me as a gamble, though, since there's a strong probability that the last thing you see on this earth is your ball veering into the trees, or bouncing into a bunker or rolling back into a stream. Purgatory must be full of golfers who just want to go back and play that shot again.

# HOW TO GET MORE DISTANCE FROM THE TEE

For some golfers, yardage is everything. Even in countries that use the metric system. Personally, I'm one of those who believe size isn't important, it's where you put it that matters. And that applies to your tee shots too. A little finesse goes a long way. But not, I admit, as far as one of those woods with a head like a football. If you're one of those golfers who isn't happy unless you can outdrive your opponent, there are several ways you can get more distance from your tee shots.

## 1 Small-bore Cannon

**Pros:**
Excellent yardage
Relatively accurate

**Cons:**
Heavy to carry around the course
Noisy

## 2 Trebuchet

**Pros:**
Good yardage
Relatively quiet

**Cons:**
Cumbersome
Requires more than one man to load

## 3 Dog

**Pros:**
Easy to transport
Enthusiastic

**Cons:**
Expensive to feed
Undiscriminating

## TIP

### FIFTY FIFTY

If you always get off to a bad start by losing the toss, change your luck by deciding as normal whether you think it's going to be heads or tails, then calling the opposite.

## RECORD BREAKERS

### LONGEST ROUND

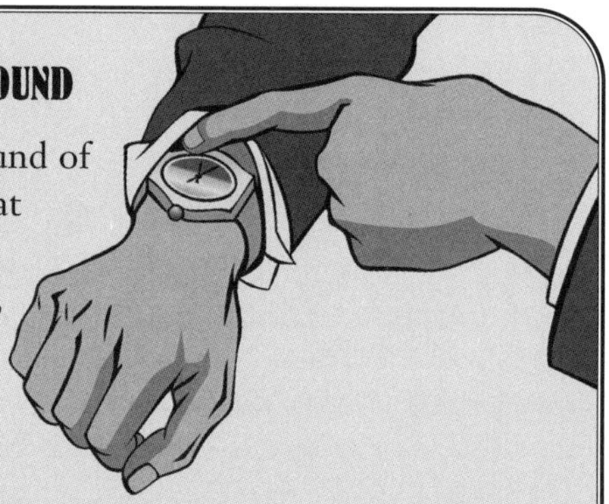

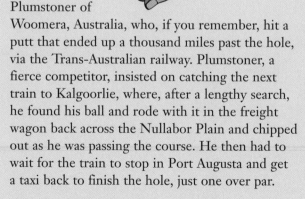

The longest round of golf was timed at 3 days, 2 hours and 21 minutes, the second of two records held by Rick Plumstoner of Woomera, Australia, who, if you remember, hit a putt that ended up a thousand miles past the hole, via the Trans-Australian railway. Plumstoner, a fierce competitor, insisted on catching the next train to Kalgoorlie, where, after a lengthy search, he found his ball and rode with it in the freight wagon back across the Nullabor Plain and chipped out as he was passing the course. He then had to wait for the train to stop in Port Augusta and get a taxi back to finish the hole, just one over par.

# GOLF GADGETS

## No.6 The Ecoclub

Not many golfers have one of these. In fact, I invented it. Well, I thought it up – it doesn't actually exist. But today's daft idea is tomorrow's Sinclair C5, as the saying goes, so I'm not giving up on it.

Everyone's looking for new sources of energy these days. Having watched a lot of golfers, it struck me that the energy they put into their shots isn't always matched by the energy that comes out. Therefore, it must be going somewhere. The Ecoclub collects it and converts it into electricity. If my calculations are correct, one round of golf will produce enough current to illuminate the Eiffel Tower for two minutes.

# CHARACTERS TO AVOID

## No.9 The Show-off

Golf naturally attracts Show-offs. The dress code permits them to be more fashionable than everyone else; the equipment invites them to be more state of the art; the rulebook allows them to be more knowledgeable; and the game itself gives them the stage on which to perform. Anyone with a pathological hunger for attention is drawn to golf like an actor to a light.

Like the Novice, you will hear them before you see them.

> 'I GOT A HOLE IN ONE THE OTHER DAY... I SHOULDN'T BRAG ABOUT IT BUT IT WAS ON A PAR 5!'
>
> 'DO YOU LIKE MY SHOES? HANDSTITCHED KOMODO DRAGON SKIN. ONLY TWO PAIRS IN THE WORLD. TIGER'S GOT THE OTHER.'
>
> 'OH SPLENDID DRIVE! ALMOST AS FAR AS MINE.'

The most annoying thing about Show-offs is that they always seem to thrive. Every time a new driver comes out with a bigger head than anything before, they're the first to get one – and it works for them. This is a chicken-and-egg question: do they show off because they're successful, or are they successful because they show off? Don't waste too much time finding out.

# BIRDIES, EAGLES, ALLIGATORS…

I was playing with a fruit pie magnate in Florida once, when an alligator emerged from the swamp, ambled across the fairway, swallowed his ball in one gulp and ambled back to its watery lair. We scratched our heads for a while and were about to declare an unplayable lie and a free drop, when the gator reappeared, further back towards the tee, and coughed up the ball in the deep rough.

'Guess he doesn't like Titleist,' I quipped. My attempt at levity didn't go down well with the pie man, who was forced to play out sideways and ended up with a double bogey. He stormed off the green swearing, 'If I see that gator again, I'll…' Apparently he did the following week. It ate him, thereby ruining another promising round.

Wildlife on the course is a common hazard for the golfer. The key is not to let it spoil your game. Here are some handy hints:

## Snakes

Most snakes see a golf club as a potential mate (their eyesight's not so great, you see). Offer it something you don't really need, like your driver, and while it's getting amorous, play on. You can come back for the club when the passion's over.

## Buffaloes

Anything that comes in gangs is best avoided. If your approach to the green is obstructed by grazing animals, you're entitled to a free drop either side of the herd but no nearer the hole. If you're already on the green, mark your ball and wait for the stampede to pass.

## Bees

Bees are attracted to the sound of golfers' trousers rubbing together. Either remain still or walk with your legs well apart. They should move on. Whatever you do, don't try to play through them.

## Elephants

I recommend a 9-iron.

# SAYINGS THAT ORIGINATED IN GOLF

Did you know that the well-known maxim, 'You can lead a horse to water, but you can't make it drink', actually began life as a golfing proverb: 'You can lead a horse to water, but a golf ball will find its own way there.'

Many of the sayings that we use today originated as golfing adages, and when you know that, they almost begin to make sense.

***He's not as green as he's cabbage looking***
HE'S NOT ON THE GREEN, HE'S IN
THE CABBAGES LOOKING FOR IT

***Many a slip 'twixt cup and lip***
DON'T DRINK AND PUTT AT THE SAME TIME

***A miss is as good as a mile***
HE MISSED BY A MILE

***A problem shared is a problem halved***
A HOLE SHARED IS A HALF

***Better to have loved and lost than never to have loved at all***
BETTER TO HAVE PLAYED AND LOST THAN TO HAVE STAYED
HOME DOING THE WASHING

***Discretion is the better part of valour***
IF IN DOUBT, TAKE AN IRON OFF THE TEE

***Faint heart never won fair lady***
TAKE A DRIVER OFF THE TEE

*If you can't be good, be careful*
TAKE AN IRON OFF THE TEE

*Fortune favours the brave*
TAKE A DRIVER OFF THE TEE

*Familiarity breeds contempt*
I WENT IN THIS SODDING BUNKER LAST TIME

*If at first you don't succeed, try, try and try again*
YOU CAN'T TAKE A DROP OUT OF A BUNKER

*Into every life a little rain must fall*
BROLLIES UP, CHAPS!

*It's an ill wind that blows no-one any good*
Bad luck, it's been blown into the lake

*Mighty oaks from little acorns grow*
I'm sure that tree wasn't there last time

*Speak softly and carry a big stick*
Whisper on the putting green

*Still waters run deep*
That's one ball I won't be finding

*To travel hopefully is a better thing than to arrive*
Hmm, I thought I was on the green

## KNOW YOUR GOLFING ETIQUETTE

**Q** *I'm trailing by a shot with two to play when my opponent is knocked unconscious by his own ball rebounding off a tree. When he comes to he has no recollection of how many he's taken. Should I tell him?*

**A** It's every player's responsibility to keep his own score, although being knocked unconscious does militate in his favour, even if it was his own fault. However, you are within your rights to plead ignorance and force him to forfeit the hole. While it seems ungentlemanly to take advantage of an injured player, this is a competitive sport and no-one asked him to hit his ball at a tree.

# A VERSE TO GOLF

Countless golfers have been moved to write poetry about their favourite sport (though very little of their output has made it beyond the pages of some obscure website on golf poetry). I too have felt the presence of the muse on the golf course, and have expressed my emotion in this haiku.

*A ball in wet sand*

*Metal cuts the silent air*

*A ball in wet sand*

# WHY GOLF IS THE BEST SPORT

Four reasons why golf is better than any other sport.

❶ **There's no running involved.**

❷ **It's a non-contact sport.**

3 Injuries are rare.

4 Spectators are well behaved.

# WHAT GOLF TEACHES US ABOUT LIFE

'Golf is life,' as a wise man once said in a desperate attempt to justify to his wife why he was spending yet another weekend away. But he was right; there are many lessons we can learn about life in general from playing golf.

JUST BECAUSE IT WORKS ON SATURDAY, DOESN'T MEAN IT'LL WORK ON SUNDAY.

ALWAYS EXPECT THE UNEXPECTED.

THINGS CAN SUDDENLY CHANGE DIRECTION WITHOUT WARNING.

# THE 19TH

I don't have much time for girls. I don't mean I don't like girls, I just don't have time for them, once you take out the hours spent on the golf course, practice, research, travel, watching my *Dukes of Hazzard* videos, playing Sudoku and writing this book. The one time I did have a girlfriend it lasted less than a day. I asked her out for a round of golf – that was all fine, except she did have a habit of talking during my back swing and consequently beat me 4 and 3.

I offered to take her for a drink in the clubhouse, not realizing it was one of those traditional old clubs where ladies aren't allowed in the men's bar. I was forced to leave her at the door while I had my usual gin and Dubonnet and then I got chatting to the Club Captain, who had just bought himself a new Jaguar. He was keen to tell me all about this car, what it could do on the motorway and how he could get two sets of clubs in the boot and what have you, and he offered me another drink. Well, you don't refuse the Club Captain, so I accepted, and then I was obliged to buy him one back, by which time we'd been joined by a four-ball, one of whom had hit a hole in one on the 12th and was buying drinks all round. To cut a long story short, by the time I left the bar there was no sign of my girlfriend and I haven't seen or heard from her since. That's gratitude for you.

### GOLF GURU: 'YOUR PROBLEMS ARE MY GOOD FORTUNE'

**5. Money** A poor man of my acquaintance once said, 'The love of money is the root of all evil,' but I will turn that round and say, 'An aversion to money is the excuse of a weasel who can never hole the crucial putt on the 18th.' Don't be ashamed of fabulous wealth – I'm not. Not in any way.
I take great pride in making sure my wife never goes short, and of all the champion golfers who have passed through my hands, there's not one who wouldn't go along with that. Their womenfolk have never gone short either. If you want to be a winner you have to keep your eyes on the prize, and the first thing I tell any new pupil is, 'If you're not hungry for the money, you're no damned use to me.' It's the only time I allow myself to curse!

GENTLEMEN
ONLY
LADIES
FORBIDDEN

# RECORD BREAKERS

## CONSECUTIVE HOLES IN ONE

During a four day tournament in 1963, unpopular amateur golfer Grant Orange scored a hole in one at the same par 3 four days in a row. The feat was made all the more remarkable by the fact that the green was hidden from the tee by trees. However, it was later discovered that other club members had colluded in paying a local schoolboy to hide in the bushes and run out and put Orange's ball in the hole each time. Having never previously bought a drink until that week, Orange's bar bill after four days came to £157 (the price of a small house in Cornwall).

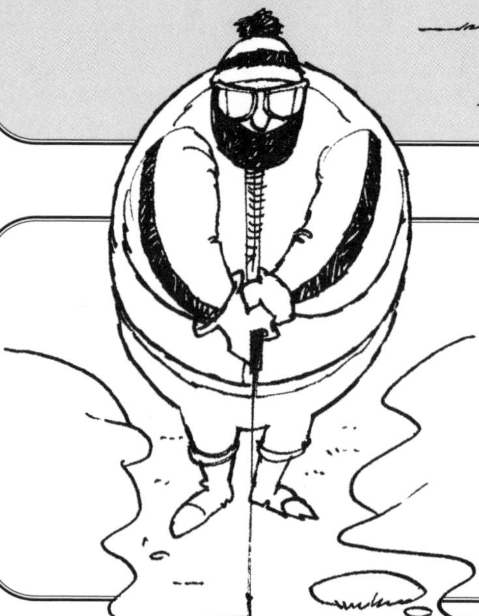

## TIP

### COLD AIN'T COOL

To prevent freezing temperatures from having an adverse effect on your golf in the winter months, wear something warmer.